HEALING THROUGH AYURVEDA

HEALING THROUGH AYURVEDA

TIPS FOR DOSHA UNDERSTANDING AND SELF CARE

SONICA KRISHAN

RUPA

First Published by
Rupa Publications India Pvt. Ltd 2011
161-B/4, Gulmohar House,
Yusuf Sarai Community Centre,
New Delhi 110049

Sales centres:
Bengaluru Chennai
Hyderabad Kolkata Mumbai

ISBN: 978-81-291-1771-7

Third impression 2026

10 9 8 7 6 5 4 3

Printed in India

This book is dedicated to my loving family.
Their love and support helped me identify, understand
and take care of the three distinct personality types
within me and all around me.

Contents

Foreword

Ayurveda dates back more than 5,000 years. The first written records of Ayurveda have been found in the Vedas, the oldest and the largest body of knowledge in history. This science of life started as an oral tradition, with the knowledge being passed down by the *rishis*, who studied nature and its laws, and analysed their effect on human beings. Extensive research and writings on Ayurveda have taken place right from the ancient times. One can even find texts on Ayurvedic surgery. *Charaka-Samhita*, one of the earliest and most authoritative texts on Ayurveda, is till date considered an important source of medical understanding and treatments. The compendium explains everything about Ayurveda, from the theory and philosophy to the cellular structure of the body and more. During the ancient times, Ayurvedic knowledge had prolifically spread to many parts of the world. Eventually, it made its way to Greece, where it had profound influence on the development of medicine. However, its use declined after the 15th century, when India came under the influence of European colonisation. In 1835 the British imposed a ban on Ayurveda in order to favour European medicine. But in the beginning of the 20th century when the struggle for India's independence gained momentum, the science of Ayurveda was revived, duly recognised and successfully practised by many Indians. At present, Ayurveda has gained back its prominence in India, and is also included in the curriculum of schools and universities.

Rigveda glorifies the importance of charity. It states that the best way to give is to expect nothing in return; and that the manner of giving is through love, devotion and respect. Imparting knowledge is the most refined form of charity as knowledge cannot be stolen or destroyed, and with time it only grows to give more happiness to everyone around. I am grateful to all those who are involved in spreading across this ancient wisdom of Ayurveda. Dr Sonica Krishan has shared a very powerful insight with us through the medium of her book *Healing Through Ayurveda – Tips For Dosha Understanding and Self Care.*

Ayurveda, being 'The Science of Life', explains the nature of everything in the universe. When we understand how the universe works, we begin to understand our place and role in the world. We begin to realise that when we keep ourselves in balance, allowing our basic nature to come sparkling through, then we attain the healthiest and happiest state. We can express ourselves clearly and confidently, with passion and purpose, in all that we do.

As we learn about Ayurveda, we get a firsthand experience of the interconnectedness of all life forms. We learn about nature, we learn about each other and also, how we can best take care of ourselves.

We are able to recognise perfection and beauty all around us. We see that every creature has a distinct role to play. The eagle is no more important than the swan. The swan is no more important than the hummingbird. We neither see the eagle wishing to be a swan, nor the swan longing to be like a hummingbird. And yet, as humans, we try to be what we are not, or expect other people to behave in ways that are contrary to their own nature and instincts.

Ayurveda teaches us that all, which is easy and effortless, is natural. This knowledge allows us to love and accept things as they are rather than crib for something that is not feasible. Living a life in balance and harmony provides us prosperity in all aspects of life: health, relationship, career, and lifestyle.

I encourage you to soak up the wisdom imparted by Dr Krishan through this highly useful book. Hope you'll reap great benefits from the science of Ayurveda and attain a fruitful combination of healthy body, mind, and spirit!

Lissa Coffey
(Author of the bestselling
health book *What's Your Dosha Baby?*)

Acknowledgements

- First and foremost my humble prayers and gratitude to the almighty, Sai Baba, who has blessed me with the ability to understand, write and spread the comprehensive knowledge of ancient Indian science of Ayurveda to the world.
- I am full of reverence for all true believers of natural means of healing and living and for all my readers who acknowledge and support the natural wisdom of health and longevity.
- I am grateful to my publisher Rupa Publications India Pvt. Ltd. for once more accepting my work and guiding me in my venture as an author.
- I thank my husband C.A. Alok Krishan for being greatly supportive and encouraging all through my endeavour.
- Heartfelt thanks to both my kids Ishita and Ishan, who have been remarkably considerate throughout my busy writing schedules. Especially Ishita, I want to thank you dear daughter as you have been part of deciding the layout of this book.
- My parents, Dr P.R. Sharma and Meera Sharma, and my mother-in-law Usha Sharma, who have always blessed me

and earnestly appreciated and motivated me throughout.
- Also, thank you Asha Sharma (*Masi*), for guiding me in the yoga techniques to align the three personalities.

All comments and feedback about the book would be genuinely valued and may please be sent at drsonica@herboveda.co.in

Preface

There is only one person in this world who knows you in the best possible manner, who knows you exactly how you are. And that is you – yourself.

We know ourselves too well, more than any other person and naturally we are aware of our shortcomings also, better than anyone else. Every individual is his/her own best friend and also his/her own worst critic. Silently and secretly, many a time we dread and suffer the limitations of our basic nature. It requires courage to realise and learn about one's shortcomings. At times it's even scary. We often wonder whether we should blame ourselves all the time for being fond of sweets, for having the tendency to put on extra pounds, for being outspoken, or for being judgmental over issues that would not actually bother us emotionally. At times we simply give in by holding ourselves responsible, at other times we feel helpless and fail to figure out why we are like that. Why do we behave in a certain manner? Why are our habits and ways different from other people? I'm sure you must have definitely pondered over this more often than you can remember. I also realise that you have not always been able to find a satisfactory answer to it. Here I bring you the good news that India's age-old science of Ayurveda has the answer to such very important queries of our life.

This book will place before you a concise essence of the science of Ayurveda that will help you find answers to all the questions that have often bothered you on a subconscious level.

- How are we formed or how did we come into existence?
- Why are all human beings not the same, and what brings about the differences in their physical appearance and temperament?
- What actually governs our basic constitution?
- Despite following most of the prescribed 'Health Rules', how come we still seem to lose our wellness every now and then?
- And last but not the least, when and how, can our natural health be restored?

As we go into all these details and get the desired answers, we will also discover and understand our natural entity, so that we can be our own lifelong guides! This is because assessing your basic and inborn nature at first helps you to accept yourself, so that you can thereafter aptly and accordingly make changes in your lifestyle. Consequently, it is perhaps the only therapy you need – in both curative as well as preventive terms – to enjoy till the last breath a life full of natural wellness and freedom from disease. I feel this surely is the need of the times.

Introduction

To attain all the aforesaid, the very first step is to be sure of the physical and mental constitution to which you belong. Only then you can move towards the second and the final step of balancing yourself in accordance with your complete entity. Let me tell you that every single interaction between yourself and the environment does matter. Whatever you eat, like, think, do, smell, touch, listen, watch and take in, affects your balance. This is because 'like increases like'

It is surprising that although we are all very much human, we are still so divergent. It is to be understood that though two people may be dissimilar in so many ways (in terms of physical features, tastes, thought process, circumstances), it is still possible to derive health and happiness following the same rules of wellness!

Though health and fitness awareness is increasing today, we are left feeling confused. One day we are told that three meals a day is sufficient diet and next day another theory of grazing every two hours becomes popular. Some fitness Guru reveals the best possible method of conditioning your body is only by gym cardio schedules, then there are those who swear by ancient yoga techniques. In general, nowadays, the lay man is left baffled. He is unable to decide which options to follow from his endless list of health mantras. Is drinking ten glasses of water everyday actually necessary or following a sleep pattern or avoiding spicy meals important? Should we be opting for meditation to combat stress? The list goes on and on. All this simply adds to our confusion and we do not gain effectively in terms of health and longevity.

The basic Ayurveda philosophy states that our total existence is governed by Nature, because our minutest component is natural. So living a life that is naturally balanced and acceptable to our own basic innate constitution is what begets physical, mental and spiritual health and longevity.

Now you would like to know first of all, how and why we categorise ourselves as products of Nature. To answer this, let me remind you that just like the entire Nature, we are all made out of five basic elements: *aakasha* or the ether, *vayu* or the air, *tejas* or the fire, *jala* or the water and *prithvi* or the earth. The ether represents the empty space between your body organs, inside the ears, in the minute cells, etc. The air element imparts all the movement that we experience like breathing, blinking of the eyes, working of our body organs and also our mobility. Fire, in our body is represented by the metabolic heat, gastric heat, body temperature, etc. Water in the body is present in form of saliva, blood, plasma, various secretions and digestive juices. The earth element makes up all matter within us, like muscles, bones, tendons, ligaments, and everything else that adds to the body substance.

Now the question gets all the more complicated that all though we are all made from the same natural stuff, then why the divergence?

To answer this, let me unfold the basis of the Ayurveda theory that although human body is *Panchabhootic*, yet the *panchbhootas* or the five elements are not existent in the same proportion in all the individuals. In fact, right from the time of birth, these fundamental elements merge in various proportions that result in the formation of varied bodily persona and mental traits.

Of the five elements, when ether and air elements combine together, it gives rise to *vatta* type or let me call it as TYPE – V personality.

The second distinct personality is a result of the fire. This is the *pitta* or TYPE – P personality.

Yet there is another type that emerges from the combining of the water and the earth. This is *kapha* type or TYPE – K personage.

While these are the three basic types that are by and large reflected in an individual's distinctiveness, combination traits are not rare either. As for instance, there may be mixing of air or ether elements with fire, resulting in the development of *vatta-pitta* personality. Or when fire tends to combine with water and/or earth, then *pitta-kapha* type is formed. Likewise, there may be in an individual, combination of water and earth components mixing together with air and ether. This forms the typical *vatta-kapha* type. Very rarely the three humors – air, fire and phlegm – coexist in an individual, who gets to be *vatta-pitta-kapha* type with varied characteristics of the three basic humors and all the five building blocks.

More aptly you need to understand the three distinct TYPE – V, P and K personalities with which you may identify yourself. Before I take you to the main part of the book, just keep the following in mind:

- Your physical as well as mental constitution is inborn and governs you throughout your life.
- Your basic constitution that pertinently defines your personality cannot undergo change.
- You can only make adaptive lifestyle changes to keep in equilibrium with your innate nature.
- You may be either the possessor of TYPE – V, TYPE – P or TYPE – K personality.
- Or you may be a combination type wherein there is equal dominance of *vatta*, *pitta* and /or *kapha*.

This book deals with the three distinct elements that are present within all of us. These three elements shape our personality. The one dosha which is dominant in an individual makes up for his or her personality. Thus the need arises first to identify yourself as to what type of personality you seem to belong. Or in other words, let it become relevant as to which particular *dosha* (*vatta*, *pitta* or *kapha*) is dominant within your body and mind; and that tends to rule your very existence.

Then, once you have acknowledged your basic persona, you need to understand why you are so. This would incur acceptance of complete understanding of oneself. Last but not the least comes the need of self-care. It would be of great help to lay down and abide by the health rules all for your own self.

In order to regain as well as restore health and wisdom, it is highly significant that we acknowledge our entity based on these three levels.

In accordance with the three distinct personalities, each has been dealt with in detail featuring four sub-parts. The first deals with identifying oneself by virtue of the dominant dosha.

The second part relates to understanding and accepting the traits that are naturally imbibed within your system. This helps you understand how and why the imbalance sets in your body and mind, and lays the foundation of the ailment that you are or might be experiencing.

Third comes the part that tells you how to take proper care of yourself by means of suitable diet and lifestyle measures.

The fourth part is the self-help guide to aid you better according to your very existence.

1. SELF-IDENTIFICATION

In this world, as you notice people around you, you are bound to sense the difference. This may at times comfort you, elude you or even shock you, but the difference prevails. In the process of surviving modestly in any circumstance that involves your interaction with other humans (there is essentially no escape), you tend to feel the disparity yet further. First and foremost thing you need to do is to discover your own self. Self-identification is one of the best tools that the ancient wisdom of Ayurveda offers. As you go through the book, you would know how you can judge and categorise the personality to which you holistically adhere. There are virtually three basic persona types, viz., *vatta* type or TYPE - V, *pitta* type or the TYPE - P and the *kapha* type or TYPE - K personalities. These are the ectomorph, mesomorph and endomorph people you see all around. Ayurveda strongly advocates the philosophy of 'As is within, so is without.' All the traits are naturally held by the doshas – *vatta*, *pitta* and *kapha*. This definitely makes up your basic nature (physical and mental aspects). You would naturally be erratic like *vatta* or the air, infuriated like *pitta* or the fire or unwavering like *kapha* or the phlegm. This happens naturally and there is nothing much you can do about it. But at the same time, you can accomplish a lot when you learn to accept and rightly manipulate your total existence providing the right comfort. First identify yourself. You will fall into one of the three distinct categorised personalities of TYPES - V, P or K. All you need to do is simply follow the traits and match them with your physique and mental temperament. For this purpose, you may refer to the personality guide that is included in the concluding part of the book. Although this seems easy, let me caution you here, dear reader, that you are bound to get confused. This is because as you go through the detailed features of all three personalities, it is a sure possibility that you find yourself matching to all the three types in some sphere or the other. It will be at this stage that the Self-identification Questionnaire will come to the rescue.

I have to state here that it has been made apparent that other than the three basic personalities, there are fusions or mixed type that are all the more common. So, you may be *vatta-pitta* type, *vatta–kapha* type or *pitta–kapha* type. Or there may rarely be individuals supporting all three basic doshas.

This book deals in detail with the three distinct personalities, TYPES – V, P and K and as you refer to the questionnaire, you may more easily evaluate yourself discovering the basic dosha that is dominant within you. And in case you score with one dosha dominating the body and the other governing your mind, then it is suggested that you consider supremacy in the physical characteristics in order to identify your fundamental existence.

2. SELF-UNDERSTANDING

To understand yourself is immensely relevant as this reveals response to queries like why you are the way you are and also what are the factors that every now and then impel you to be at discomfort with your being. That's right, even before the doctor, who after observing your symptoms and medical reports, relates you to some particular ailment, it is you and only you who can be aware of the imbalance when it first begins to torment your system. Previously, we have understood that as per the theory of 'like attracts like', one is more likely to appeal towards that element which is already within. One is more likely to be attracted towards the properties that already reign within the person. To make it simple, let us say that in case you are TYPE – V, the air humor within you would always impart a pull towards meagre eating, and your liking would be more for a lifestyle with being over-active. But if you are more of a TYPE – P kind, you would just by default be judgmental and obsessed. You might find it hard to resist getting into antagonism every now and then. If you are TYPE – K, then your desirability would be towards sweet foods and sedentary routine.

It is clear now that by the 'Similars Attract' phenomenon, Ayurveda has answers to how and why you lose wellness. It is under the spell of the basic dosha which dominates your system that you are particularly tempted to lead a specific lifestyle and eat just in accordance with that basic dosha. What is going to happen then? Surely if you tend to add to something that is already supple, then it will result in excess of it. This is another relevant scientific theory – 'Like Increases Like.'

Increase of the *vatta* dosha promptly affects and imbalances the TYPE – V personality. Similarly, increase in *pitta* and *kapha* would naturally result in the imbalance of TYPE – P and TYPE – K, respectively.

Imbalance is precisely the first stage of disease formation. This shows that the vitiated humors have started producing some distinct signs, which many a time go unnoticed. Yet according to Ayurveda, these signs of imbalance should not be neglected but noticed and observed very carefully. This is because, at this stage, the humor imbalance can be corrected easily and the balance can be restored. On the contrary, once the imbalanced humor traverses this stage, it tends to manifest deeper in body tissues *(dhatus)*, organs, extremities (*shakha*) and furthermore in the channels *(srotas)*. As the stage advances, it becomes all the more pathetic and difficult to cure.

Even so, whenever an ailment takes form, the primary cause is the imbalanced dosha. Therefore, balancing the dosha (*vatta*, *pitta* or *kapha*) is the only way that can help in combating the ailment, and restoring wellness.

It is apparent as per Ayurveda that imbalance of the air humor results in production of eighty types of diseases or disorders. Whereas the imbalance of fire can cause forty types of disorders, phlegm would stand responsible for twenty types of ailments.

We need to first know exactly which of the three humors dictate our physical and mental entity. This indirectly reveals to us the basic constitution and temperament to which we belong.

Then we can take a more serious note of the maladies that the vitiation or aggravation of either of the humors is bound to present itself, or in many cases we might have already frequented some of these.

It can also be understood that the basic type of humor we belong to, can be more easily verified as we take notice of the relative ailments, and at the same time this is also a word of caution to forego the afflictions that might sooner or later set in and cause unnecessary distress.

3. SELF CARE

In this part of the book, we learn by the Ayurveda way, how we can actually keep the humor (*vatta*, *pitta* or *kapha*) in balance and know more about what suits our basic personality TYPES – V, P or K.

Also find out more about the small routine transitions in your diet and lifestyle which would not only help cure but also take care of your elemental constitutions for the lifetime!

All the three vitiated or imbalanced humors can be brought back to their original form. The only principle that works in this regard is to bring about a change in the *aahara* (diet pattern) and in the *vihara* (everyday activities that make your lifestyle). It has been specifically acknowledged in Ayurveda text that a dosha or body humor tends to get aggravated mainly by undertaking aahara and vihara of the properties similar to the respective doshas. This is because 'like increases like'. Hence the vitiated or aggravated dosha can only be nullified by undertaking the diet regimen and activities which oppose that particular humor in properties.

The Ayurveda approach to restore the balance would be to make use of diet, medicine, therapy and lifestyle, all in contrasting properties of the aggravated humor so as to alleviate the same and vice versa.

4. SELF-HELP GUIDE FOR YOUR PERSONALITY (TYPES – V, P OR K)

After you ascertain and acknowledge the particular humor or humors that dominate your existence, you will also be able to learn why you have occasional bouts of anger over petty issues (TYPE –P), suffer guilt pangs as you tend to overeat and laze out (TYPE – K), or are tired of quenching your dry skin with a world of creams and oily preparations (TYPE – V). So, it is all rooted in your basic entity and so you cannot do much about it. Yet at the same time, however complicated the subject, there are a few summarised suggestions that could be of great help without fumbling about unnecessary medications and anxiety.

These have been furthermore put in tabloid form.

Part One

1 TYPE – V Personality (The *vatta* type)

I. SELF-IDENTIFICATION

You may discover yourself as holding typical *vatta* traits or the TYPE – V personality in case most of the following attributes match your entity:

1. You have a thin and lean physique and tend to walk notably fast.
2. Normally you have a rough and dry texture of skin and keep getting fissures on soles of feet and in palms and your skin tends to wrinkle early. Also, the texture of your hair might be rather parched and coarse, and hair growth, sparse.
3. You seem to have a comparatively darker complexion and your body may be marked with prominent veins.
4. The nails are rough and get cracked easily and tend to be dark in colour.
5. Teeth are generally uneven, fragile and more prone to dental cavities and plaque.
6. You are really fond of music and tend to talk much, sometimes irrelevant.
7. Cool of the winters or cold environments are just unbearable for your being.

8. You are a rapid eater and usually find it difficult to set proper timings and regulations for taking meals.
9. There is a general feeling of restlessness and anxiety in your being which gets aggravated by external stimuli, and your eyes blink a lot.
10. You seem to grasp an idea quickly but find it hard to retain the same.
11. Your sexual needs and capacity for enjoyment is somehow meagre.
12. Emotionally you might not easily rely on friendships and relations, and small things hurt and bring resentment.
13. A weak memory and fluctuating mental attitude prevails especially at the time of decision-making.
14. In dreams, you may find yourself scaling the skies.
15. You are more often affected by maladies like muscular cramps, joint pains and stiffness, nervous weakness, abdominal gas, constipated bowels, improper sleep, etc.
16. Mentally you are afflicted by occasional depressive moods, emotional fluctuations and indecisiveness.

Broadly, this type of *prakriti* or the innate nature would reflect those very qualities that are present in the *vatta* or the air.

Air by its very nature is dry, light, cold, subtle, raw and transparent. And in case your body has more of *vatta*, you are sure to imbibe these properties within your very identity. Let me now illustrate how the TYPE – V individuals reflect the basic traits of the air.

Vatta or the air is:

1. *Ruksha* (dry, rough). So the skin and hair are dry and rough.
2. *Laghu* (light). The person will have light bony structure, would be devoid of fat. He/she would be a frivolous thinker, with an often fluctuating mental state. He has a light sleep.

3. *Shita* (cold). *Vatta* person is generally unable to tolerate colder climates and seeks comfort in warmth.
4. *Sukshma* (fine, subtle). This makes the TYPE – V person erratic in temperament as he/she jumps to new ideas frequently.
5. *Khara* (raw, loose). The joints, muscles and tendons are devoid of firmness. The person's joints may produce sound on movement.
6. *Vishada* (clear, transparent). This property makes the person anxious and more prone to getting influenced.

However, *rajas guna* makes the TYPE – V mentally creative, stimulated and flexible.

II. SELF-UNDERSTANDING

Let us understand how TYPE – V or the *vatta* individuals are typical of their basic nature.

As the air manifests and dominates within the being of the TYPE – V person right from the time of birth, the bodily features, as well as the mental disposition may be attributed to the excess of the air humor residing in the body. Subsequently as is the air (not to forget that this humor is further made from natural elements of ether and air), so is the individual holding analogous qualities.

A person having TYPE – V personality would normally be thin, tall and somewhat hideous. The body parts lack stability and might show jerky movements. Veins and tendons are superfluously observable. Skin is dark, dry and prone to wear and tear. The hair is parched and brittle. Eyes seem to be generally repulsive and protruding while the person is asleep. Voice is hoarse. The individual with TYPE – V nature walks fast, and on moving his joints make sound. He eats less and prefers food items that are spicy, salty or sour in taste. Due to the cold property of *vatta*, this person cannot tolerate cold climates. Also, his physical strength and stamina are, in general, relatively less.

The individual is always fast in action. He grasps very fast but also soon forgets the same due to his low levels of intellect and short memory powers. He talks a lot but his nature is never stable. He lacks patience, remains restless and is simply incapable of showing much devotion towards friends and relations. In demanding times, he will suddenly go into sessions of depression and agony, and will want to be left alone. He will swiftly then spring back into action and desire solace in supportive company. By nature, he might be a non-believer in god.

The positive TYPE – V traits are that the person is very creative, manipulative, vibrant and full of zeal. *Vatta* individuals are also great thinkers.

As for the negative TYPE – V traits, this individual could be covetous, coward and immoral. His mental temperament is that of *rajas* type as he would keep grieving even without a reason. On the whole, just like the air, he remains mentally unstable. He dreams more of high mountains, heights, tall trees and often sees himself flying in the sky.

It is mainly the erratic nature of air humor which actually makes *vatta* individuals lack stability both in mind as well as body.

Imbalance in TYPE – V

Vatta gets naturally aggravated during old age, in the late evenings, during cloudy skies especially in the rainy season, and after taking meals.

Eventually, other reasons that would aggravate *vatta* and throw the TYPE – V people out of equilibrium both physically and also mentally, largely relate to two factors explicitly — diet and lifestyle.

The diet imbalance in TYPE – V

1. More intake of foodstuffs that are light, cold and dry by nature increases this particular humor.

2. Fasting for longer periods or meagre ingestion of food.
3. *Vatta* imbalance in the TYPE – V individuals may also arise from the intake of bitter, pungent and astringent foodstuff.

The lifestyle imbalance in TYPE – V

1. Habitual suppression of natural urges like passing stool, urination, passing wind, belching, etc. (There are thirteen un-suppressible natural urges).
2. More exposure to cold climates or cold, dry winds.
3. Less sleeping hours or ignoring or delaying the call of sleep.
4. Keeping mentally alert or anxious due to unaccountable fears.
5. Taking up routines of long brisk walks or heavy exercises.
6. Working without rest and ignoring the body's need to take a break both physically as well as mentally.
7. Talking a lot and giving very little rest to the vocal cords.
8. Accidental traumas like falling from height, fractures, etc.

Now when we know the reasons that aggravate *vatta* and furthermore cause imbalance in TYPE – V person, we must also be aware of the logic behind it.

Vatta would easily fall out of balance and aggravate with anything that is undertaken (diet and lifestyle) that resembles the basic characteristics of the air humor. Remember 'like increases like'. When you eat or undertake your everyday activities, when you have precisely matched your qualities with *vatta* and identified yourself to be TYPE – V kind, then you should understand how knowingly or unknowingly you add to the traits within your system. *Vatta* easily falls out of balance when you tend to eat Vattagenic (*vatta* increasing) diet and undertake all those activities in your everyday lifestyle that match the natural traits of air-body humor. This means, in case you are a *vatta*-dominant (TYPE – V) personality with already more of *vatta* in your system, you need to understand that, knowingly or unknowingly, you might be augmenting the humor within you by enhancing the *vatta* traits by the means of daily diet and lifestyle.

1. *Ruksha* – dry, rough. Taking arid and dry foods and living in dry weather conditions.
2. *Laghu* – light. Taking meagre meals, fasting or holding on to hunger, foods that supposedly have high air content, aerated drinks.
3. *Shita* – cold, cooling. Cold, frozen foods and drinks, living in cold environment.
4. *Sukshma* – fine, subtle, penetrating. Restraining on the natural urges and often changing moods with less of mental concentration on a single subject.
5. *Khara* – raw, loose. Rushing with body parts, uncontrolled speech, excess physical exercise forceful on the joints and bones.
6. *Vishada* – clear, not viscous, transparent. Sudden intense changes in life, seasonal changes, mood swings.

The mental discrepancy of *rajas guna* to remain in state of anxiety, nervousness and apprehension also vitiates *vatta.*

It is probably clear that an ailment transpires from imbalance. And imbalance results mainly from improper diet and inappropriate lifestyle. And the reason for all this is also apparent as alike qualities attract and also augment. As we are going through the section on self-understanding, it must be known especially to TYPE – V individuals what happens when *vatta* aggravation causes imbalance within their system.

Signs of Imbalance in TYPE – V

Aggravation of the *vatta* or the air humor in the body is considered more perilous than the aggravation of other two humors. This is because of the erratic and unstable natural trait of this dosha. So if you are TYPE – V with more of *vatta* in your system, you need to be more cautious as you could be effortlessly thrown out of balance. Watch for some signs that could specify *vatta* imbalance:

1. The skin becomes more rough and rugged.
2. There is continuous feeling of lethargy or lassitude.
3. Restlessness or impatience is more.
4. Muscular cramps and body aches are on the rise.
5. Difficulty in having sound sleep.
6. Gas formation or belching is more.
7. Constipated motion.
8. There might be stiffness or trembling of body parts.
9. There is aversion from cold, and the body naturally demands warm food and environment.
10. Mentally, there are obvious signs of frequent inability to memorise. Fearfulness, nervousness and sometimes depression might prevail.
11. Anxiety or fears exist.
12. Ayurveda implies the mental discrepancy of *vatta* imbalance as the failure of retention.

Eighty ailments that may be encountered by TYPE – V

1. *Nakha bheda* – Cracking of the nails
2. *Vipadika* – Cracking of the soles of the feet
3. *Padashula* – Pain of the feet
4. *Padabhramsha* – Steps do not fall at the right place while walking, flat foot
5. *Padasupta* – Numbness of the feet
6. *Vatakhuddata* – Pain in the hip joint
7. *Gulphagraha* –Sprain or stiffness of the ankle
8. *Pindikovestana* – Cramp in the calf region

9. *Gridhrasi* – Sciatica
10. *Janubheda* – Bow legs
11. *Januvilesha* – Knock knees
12. *Urustamba* – Stiffness or paralysis of the thigh
13. *Urusada* – Pain in the thighs due to atrophy of thigh muscles
14. *Pangulya* – Lameness or deformed foot
15. *Gudabhramsa* – Prolapsed anus
16. *Gudarti* – Pain and tenesmus in the anal region
17. *Vrishnotksepa* – Pain in the testis or in the scrotal area
18. *Sophasthamba* – Stiffness of the penis
19. *Vanksanabha* – Tension in the groin
20. *Sronibheda* – Pain around the pelvic girdle
21. *Vibheda* – Loose motions
22. *Udavrata* – Paralysis of the intestines
23. *Khanjatva* – Lameness
24. *Kubjatva* – Hunchback
25. *Vamanatva* – Dwarfness
26. *Trikagraha* – Arthritis of the sacro-iliac joint, Neuralgic pain in the sacral region
27. *Pristhagraha* – Stiffness of the back
28. *Prasva vamarda* – Pain in the chest along with difficulty in breathing
29. *Udaravesta* – Gripping pain in the abdomen
30. *Hrinmoha* – Heart block, heart failure or Cardiac inactivity
31. *Hriddrava* – Palpitations, Tachycardia
32. *Vakshaudgarsa* – Pain in the chest
33. *Vakshauparodha* – Damage of the thoracic movement
34. *Vakshastoda* – Stabbing pain in the chest
35. *Vahushosha* – Atrophy of the arm
36. *Grivastambha* – Stiffness of the neck
37. *Kathoddhvamsa* – Hoarseness of the voice
38. *Hanubheda* – Dislocation of the jaw with severe pain

39. *Manyastambha* - Spasmodic contraction of neck muscles causing stiffness of the neck on one side
40. *Osthabheda* - Pain and tearing in the lips
41. *Akshibheda* - Pain in the eyes
42. *Dantabheda* - Pain in the teeth
43. *Dantashaithalya* - Looseness of the teeth
44. *Mukhatva* - Dumbness
45. *Vaksanga* - Impaired speech
46. *Kshayasyata* - Astringent taste in the mouth
47. *Mukhshosha* - Dryness of the mouth
48. *Arasagyata* - Loss of taste
49. *Granananasha* - Anosmia
50. *Karnashoola* - Pain in the ears
51. *Ashabdashravana* - Tinnitus
52. *Ucchaisruti* - Hard of hearing
53. *Bhadirya* - Deafness
54. *Vartma samkocha* - Retraction of the eyelids
55. *Vartma stambha* - Rigidity of the eyelids
56. *Akshiyudasa* - Eyeballs raised upwards
57. *Timira* - Partial loss of vision
58. *Bhruvyudasa* - Eyebrows raised upwards
59. *Shankabheda* - Headache with pain in the temporal area, Migraine
60. *Lalatabheda* - Headache with pain in the frontal area
61. *Siroruk* - Headache
62. *Kesabhumi sphutana* - Fissures in the scalp, dandruff
63. *Ardita* - Facial paralysis
64. *Ekanga Roga* - Monoplegia
65. *Pakshavyadha* - Hemiplagia
66. *Sarvanga Roga* - Paralysis, Paraplegia
67. *Akshepa* - Clonic convulsions
68. *Dandaka* - Tonic convulsions
69. *Shrama* - Excessive tiredness

70. *Vepathu* - Tremors
71. *Jrimbha* - Yawning
72. *Hikka* - Hiccups
73. *Bhrama* - Giddiness
74. *Vishada* - State of unhappiness
75. *Atipralapa* - Delirium
76. *Rukshata* - Dryness
77. *Parushya* - Hardness, harshness
78. *Syavaruna dhasata* - Dusky red appearance of body or part of the body
79. *Aswapna* - Loss of sleep
80. *Anavishthita chitva* - Mental instability

III. SELF CARE

According to Ayurveda, in order to combat *vatta* imbalance, one needs to take charge of his diet and routine just like serving a close friend.

Varatam snehanam mitravata

Moreover, when dealing with *vatta* aggravation, any change in the existing scenario of the TYPE - V person needs to be subdued slowly and steadily just like taking care of a potted plant. This is because *vatta* is fragile. So if you seem to be a TYPE - V kind, you definitely need to make the ensuing transition, and yet at the same time try not being too strict and pushy with yourself; rather, it is important to guide yourself steadily with tender care.

Diet management in TYPE – V

As far as the diet of a TYPE - V person is concerned, it is imperative to be sustained at regular intervals. Keeping the stomach empty would invite aggravation of the air humor. The meals should not be too heavy, but more frequent. As opposed to the properties of *vatta* (cold, light, dry), diet that is warm, heavy and unctuous is beneficial. Food that is high in nutritive value and energy-giving helps subside the distorted humor. Some herbs like *brahmi*, *shankhpushpi* that are intellect-promoting would help in keeping the mind fixed and stable. Tastes that are apt for TYPE - V people are primarily sweet, salty and sour and the other three, i.e. bitter, pungent and astringent, need to be avoided. Intake of oil of *til* seeds (sesame seed) is also recommended to allay *vatta* and keep the distorted dosha in control.

Stimulating and digestive herbs and condiment powders if included in everyday diet help to keep the gastric fire upright. Moreover, according to Ayurveda, TYPE - V persons naturally by and large have disturbed gastric fire or *vishamagni*.

Lifestyle management in TYPE - V

'Use your head and your body will follow' – this is the most appropriate phrase for the *vatta* types. Whatever you do, you have to be first sure in your mind about the time scheduling and settlement. And you will see it for yourself that life becomes so easy to handle. When *vatta* has to be brought back into balance, it is highly commendable to foremost take up the diet and routine that oppose the traits of humor. Earlier we had perceived how similarities tend to aggravate and imbalance the dosha. Once again consider the *vatta* qualities. But this time to comprehend how to bring about the converse. All you need to do is reminisce about the properties of the air and perform in plain antagonism.

1. *Ruksha* - dry, rough. The dryness of *vatta* needs to be countered with use of oil internally as well as externally. Warm oil massage is specifically recommended. Also, as for the reason, let me remind you that oily diet is rather essential.

2. *Laghu* – light. In contrast to this property of the air, diet needs to be somewhat heavy in nature and the stomach needs to get replenished more frequently with nourishing food.
3. *Shita* – cold, cooling. So as to go against this feature, warm and freshly cooked foods with hot potency, hot fomentation of body parts and bathing in the sun would help.
4. *Sukshma* – subtle, penetrating. Relaxing attitude, regulating sleep pattern and following stability in work and environment is needed.
5. *Khara* – raw, loose. Unyielding daily schedules and managing timetable is desirable. Maintaining silence and observing periods of concentration would be of relevant help.
6. *Vishada* – clear, transparent. Contrary to this trait, avoiding undue stress and physical exertion, and eating warm thick vegetable soup with *vatta* pacifying condiments is useful.

Some more amicable suggestions for subduing *vatta* in the TYPE – V individuals could be:

1. Whole body massage with some previously warmed oil or with oil having hot potency, like mustard oil, sesame seed oil, is advised.
2. Hot fomentation of the body parts especially during cold climates.
3. Hot bandaging of body parts, warm poultice, forceful pressing of the body parts.
4. Applying manual pressure on the body and limbs with care and compassion.
5. Applying turmeric and saffron paste on the body.
6. Bathing with warm to hot water and applying the same onto the body provides relief.

7. Taking nap or resting in favourable environment without any stimuli would be of help.

As the mental state of *rajas guna* is predominant in *vatta*, the TYPE – V individuals need to focus more on the positive mental traits of *vatta* humor like creativeness, zest and flexibility. Air humor being highly erratic and poignant renders parallel effect on the mind. This is why a *vatta* person finds it impossible to remain focussed. And *vatta* is fragile and impulsive and needs to be handled with care (like a friend). All the thoughts and memories that are relaxing should be kept in mind, and fearful and anxious reflections should be firmly overlooked. Herbs that are brain tonics and supportive to central nervous system are useful.

Everything in TYPE – V lifestyle (including food intake and daily activities) needs to be organised and regularised. This is because air humor being restless and erratic all the time, tends to easily evade discipline. A person with TYPE – V personality must always keep this in mind. Almost everything in the daily routine needs to be dealt well with by following a regular time table. The bowel movement must be regular and so should be the sleep pattern. Indulgence in activities like chatting, reading or watching television at bedtime should be specially avoided. A decent sleep routine is very essential for the TYPE – V individual because the frequently dodging mind has to be kept under control.

All those activities that provide contentment and pleasure, both to mind and body, should be undertaken.

Vocal rest is a must for managing *vatta* as this humor is erratic, fast and mobile. Meditation, yoga and breathing techniques should be followed daily. Such practices help relaxing the mind as energy is conserved.

As is clear by now, air being dry, oil massage is good for TYPE – V person. Also let me tell you that even the sense of touch (out of the five senses) appeases the aggravated *vatta*. Any *vatta*-pacifying oil such as sesame seed or mustard oil (many medicinal oils are advised in Ayurveda therapy), or any previously warmed oil can be rubbed onto the body. Packs of warm herbs like saffron or *agar* can be mixed with oil and applied on the skin.

Other than warm oil massages, sun bathing is also suggested. Oiling of the body as well as therapies like steam, sauna, hot fomentation, pressing or kneading body parts with warm hands, hot tub bath and sprinkling of hot water onto the body parts (especially *vatta*-specific area below the umbilicus) helps to subside the aggravated humor.

Both body and mind should be relaxed from time to time.

Therapeutically, when *vatta* is highly imbalanced, it gives rise to the eighty types of *vatta* ailments; in that case one must go for *vasti*, a variety of *Panchkarma* therapy.

Importance of the usage of enemas has been extremely recommended so as to allay the vitiated *vatta*.

Vastivartaharana shreshtam **(*CS* Su 25/39)**

According to Ayurveda, most of the activities and diet recommended for the winter season would benefit a TYPE – V individual. Thus while narrating the regime for the winter season; the Ayurveda has rightly advocated the aahara (diet pattern) and vihara (daily activities) of a *vatta* individual. In other words, as in the cold season the weather is dry and cold, consequently Ayurveda suggests that during this particular season, we all need to have a sturdy lifestyle like that of a TYPE – V personality and vice versa.

IV. SELF-HELP GUIDE FOR TYPE – V

Diet

Diet is of foremost consideration if we need to ward off the dosha. A lot depends on taking a diet of right choice. For *vatta* types, optimal scheduling of diet programme is very important. The air humor being dry, rough, erratic and cool, may be settled if one takes diet of just the opposite traits. Therefore TYPE - V individuals need to feast more on oily, heavy and fairly warm foodstuffs. Luckily, they are also permitted to enjoy the three best tastes – sweet, salty and sour. Milk and milk products may also be included as long as these do not interfere with one's digestion (TYPE - V generally have erratic digestion). Setting appropriate time for your meals is equally essential. Also in your case and with your mostly weak digestion, it is more effective if you take small meals but at regular intervals. Overeating would be unbearable for you and on the other hand remaining completely without food may fill your stomach with gaseous discomfort. Ayurveda recommends division of the stomach into four parts: two parts are to be filled with solid food and one with liquids. And the remaining one-fourth is to be kept empty for the easy movement of gases. This principle applies aptly for the TYPE - V personalities.

Tastes

All the foods that are sweet, salty and sour in taste are suitable for the *vatta* types. And you need to substantially cut down on other three *rasas* or tastes, viz., pungent, bitter and astringent.

Herbs

There are a number of *vatta*-subsiding natural herbs which either have the suitable properties of being sour or sweet in taste or are hot in potency. Some herbs may be slimy and robust. Slimy = oily, viscous, and robust = intense and the herbs that are heavy in nature, aid in settling down the aggravated *vatta*. Holding any or all of these natural traits makes the herb useful to mitigate the aggravated *vatta* and thus comes as boon for TYPE - V persons.

Four beneficial kitchen herbs namely ginger, garlic, *ajwain* or the bishop's weed and the large cardamom have been detailed further. Other than these, you may make your choice from many more herbs like turmeric, *aamla*, holy basil, betel, black pepper, cardamom, asafoetida, etc.

Condiments

There are a variety of seasoning and condiments used in our Indian kitchens which mostly suit the TYPE - V (and TYPE - K) personalities. You may easily choose from black pepper, ginger, garlic, turmeric, liquorice, saffron, cumin, coriander, cinnamon, nutmeg, asafoetida, aniseed, fennel, bishop's weed, fenugreek, mustard, etc.

Vegetables

Vegetables that are mainly sweet, salty and sour in taste, warm in potency, or slimy and somewhat heavy by nature, would all suit the TYPE - V individuals. You may choose from most of the seasonal vegetables like onion, garlic, turnip, carrots, beans, pumpkin, lemon, drumstick, spinach, green fenugreek, asparagus, mint, bitter gourd, white gourd, bottle gourd, etc. As a *vatta* person you should take care to feast mostly on cooked or steamed vegetables, rather than those in raw state. Ground tubers like potato, sweet potato, *arbi*, etc., need to be restricted as these are believed to be Vattagenic.

Fruits

All sorts of sweet and sour fruits can be taken. Fruits that are well ripened like apples, bananas, strawberries, pineapple, papaya, *bilwa*, figs, sugarcane, coconut, mango, pomegranate, etc. While opting for nuts and dry fruits, you need to be somewhat restrictive.

Diet restriction

As it has already been stated, it is more suitable if the TYPE - V individuals include less of bitter, pungent and astringent tastes, dry, cold and very light foods in their daily diet plan. Ayurveda further constrains taking of food like white gram, red kidney bean, black gram (*sabut mah dal*), potatoes, arbi, curd, sour buttermilk and pickles as these are *vatta*-escalating.

Fasting for TYPE – V

This has been explained earlier that you being a *vatta* personality need not be abrupt or harsh with yourself at any cost. This is because you are naturally more fragile than it may seem even to yourself. It is good although if you could manage to take a break from the daily diet and give your system a complete rest. But first be clear in your mind that it is you and only you who will benefit from the fast you intend to keep. Secondly it is equally important that you set the timing for the decisive days, so you do not overdo it. This is because it might interfere with the successful result of fasting and unwillingly leave you the worse for it.

When your mind is clear and ready, then there are high chances of your accomplishing the mission effortlessly. You need not fast more often – only once a month or once a fortnight is sufficient. As a peculiar TYPE – V person you would never admit this (even to yourself) that you have no stored reservoir of energy. It is better if you simply let go of solid food but incorporate more fruits and vegetable salads mildly steamed or in the form of fresh juice. As you are allowed milk and milk products, try diluted and salted *chhaach* or buttermilk. Lemonade or diluted orange juice may also suit your fasting.

Essential oils

You may appropriately use aromatic oils as frequently as you like. Use them as few drops either burned in oil burners or mixed in your massage oil. You may also use the same mixed in your warm bath water. Many *vatta*-combating oils may be used for this purpose like eucalyptus, lavender, cinnamon, camphor or saffron oil.

Sleep pattern

The TYPE - V individuals tend to be on the move most of the time and it is rather difficult for them to sit still and relax. Also seemingly that *vatta* reasons rapidity, mobility and erratic nature both of the body as well as mind, it becomes all the more vital to get adequate sleep and relaxation. A regular sleep pattern has to be followed, even if it means to cut down on your engagements. A full 7 to 8 hours of undisturbed sleep is needed all the more so that it calms and relaxes your innately delicate nervous system. Sound sleep will refresh you and make you ready for a busy schedule the next day. For this, a previously warmed bed, a warm water bath with relaxing essential oil drops added to it, massage of legs and soles of the feet, and hot and sweetened buffalo's milk would stimulate proper and unperturbed snooze. Another technique that may be considered to standardise the *vatta* sleep is to religiously follow the sleeping position of lying straight on the back for first eight breaths, then onto the right side for the count of sixteen and subsequently thirty two breaths are to be taken lying on your left side. You may then carry on with your sleep on the left side as this promotes the right nostril breathing which is warm and comforting for you. Little day-time power naps would also add up to your mental calm.

Exercise and Yoga for TYPE – V

For the TYPE - V people, it needs to be always kept in mind that too much of activity, be it with your tongue, your body or your mind, needs to be consciously constrained. You have to save energy and for this reason, exercise or go for walks but within limits. Whenever you outdo (there are many chances you would), *vatta* is going to be thrown out of kilter.

Yoga *asanas* that are recommended for the nervous system and abdominal gas are definitely going to benefit you. You only need to be patient and regular. Some suggested yoga postures are:

1. *Bhujang Asana*
2. *Siddha Asana*
3. *Vajra Asana*
4. *Dhanur Asana*
5. *Pavanmukta Asana*
6. *Pashchimottan Asana*
7. *Hala Asana*
8. *Mandook Asana*

Some *pranayaam* or breathing techniques for TYPE – V

1. *Bhastrika Pranayaam*
2. *Anulom Vilom Pranayaam*

Mudra or hand alignment for TYPE – V

The simple hand-alignment techniques that can be practised for five to ten minutes daily are recommended for *vatta* balance.

1. *Vayu Mudra*
2. *Hridya Mudra*
3. *Dhyan Mudra*
4. *Apana Mudra*
5. *Shoonya Mudra*
6. *Gyana Mudra*

Other highly beneficial yoga *kriyas* or methods for TYPE – V

1. *Kunjal Kriya*
2. *Shankh Prakshalan*

Massage therapy

Vatta dosha may be proscribed by the sense of touch and moreover the use of oil is highly advantageous as it goes against the basic property of lightness and dryness. So TYPE – V individuals may benefit from massage as a therapy. Ayurveda suggests oils with warm to hot potency like the sesame seed oil, mustard oil or even the castor oil to be used more often and in ample quantity. *Vatta* suppressing oil that is also recommended for relieving joint pains and body stiffness like the Mahanarayan oil is available and is popular medicinal oil. The oil is first spread all over the body, especially the lower extremities and the lower abdomen (these being the main site of the air humor) and then one needs a massage with gentle touch strokes and movements of rubbing, pressing and stroking would help the oil to penetrate and as a result this would give more relief. You need to keep your mind virtually relaxed with eyes closed so as to gain the most from the massage.

Colour therapy

As a TYPE – V personality, one thought that should be kept in mind is that you are frail and subtle. It is for this reason that Ayurveda had time and again counselled that you should never undergo severity by any means. This holds true for the choice of colours that you imbibe with your eyes throughout the day. This may be in the form of the dress you wear, curtain tapestry, carpeting and the wall paints of your room, etc. You need to be fairly restrictive in using very intense and bold colours like reds, dark orange, navy blue, grey and black. Although paler and pastel shades of most of the colours would do fine. Eventually green is to be the colour of choice as and when possible. Green-charged water with sun's rays could be of great benefit as it helps in balancing the air.

Gem therapy

TYPF – V individuals can suitably benefit from the use of gem crystals like emerald, diamond, yellow sapphire and ruby. These may be used externally as ornaments of rings, bracelet or necklace (make sure they touch your skin). Also it is more comforting (and warming) to have them set in gold rather than silver. Or else you may keep the gems in a glass of water overnight and in the morning drink the gem-charged water.

Meditation

Meditation for the TYPE – V is a must for psychosomatic wellness (more vital for you than the other two personalities). The reason is that you have to master the skill managing your mind. And meditation is a complete healer not only of the mind and body, but also of the soul. The best time for you or in general for everyone is the morning *vatta* mystical time, i.e. between 2 a.m. and 6 a.m. As the sense of sound appeals to you, you will feel significantly attached to listening to *mantras* from the CD or pronouncing the same all by yourself. The sound from the properly chanted mantras emits positive energies and this is going to be of great aid. Also as for meditation, *vatta* type of persons need to try and stabilise the mind, at least for whatever time it obeys. And last but not the least, you need to fix proper timings for your meditation practice everyday. This is very important because if you do not schedule it precisely, the chances are that you would never be able to practise the bliss of meditation.

Chakra balance

In case you identify with TYPE – V individuals, then be sure that you are a sum total of the air and the ether elements. This has been detailed earlier. There are two *chakras* to which these two elements relate. One is Anahata Chakra and the other is Vishudha Chakra.

The Anahata or the heart chakra corresponds directly to the air element. This is greenish in colour and lies just at the site of the heart. This chakra is believed to be the giver of many body and mind fundamental gains. Also meditating on this chakra helps to activate the same and beget the feelings of love and spiritual gains. On the other hand, the Vishudha or the throat chakra that lies right in front of the throat and is the site for the utmost subtle aakasha or the ether element. This is blue in colour, supports the thyroid and parathyroid endocrine glands, and on spiritual grounds, promotes intellect, inner peace and emotional happiness.

Seasonal support

Vatta gets naturally aggravated in the rainy season. This is the time when the aggravation in this dosha or humor may cause easy production of eighty types of *vatta* ailments. Therefore TYPE - V people need to be immensely conscious and try to keep the dosha in balance. Even before it shows signs of aggravation, *vatta* tends to accumulate in summers. This may be apparent by noticing the dryness of this humor as it affects the vegetation. Plants and vegetables lose their moisture and tend to become drier during summers. But it is the autumn season in which the air humor gets alleviated all by itself.

Suggested hobbies and career

As you have dominance of the air within you, you need to develop hobbies that help in settling down. You may choose from anything that keeps you creative and relaxed. This can be listening to mind soothing music, enjoying massage and spa sessions, painting, spending quality time with family and friends, basking in the sun. Let it be whatever that pleases you and pacifies your strained nerves. Also it is advisable that you let go of your rationalism while you enjoy your leisure pursuit.

Now as you have inborn creativity, it would be best if you are able to use it while deciding upon a career for yourself. You may opt to become an artist, writer, architect, interior designer, dancer, actor and likewise. Just take care never to let the pressure build up as this may only kick off *vatta* imbalance.

Important norms

Everyday routines need to be maintained and regularised. Whatever you do throughout the day would become much easier and meaningful in case you are able to set proper timetable for yourself. You do not need to be ruthless and strict with yourself, but allow the necessary lifestyle changes to crawl into your life. All you would need is only to convince your mind to do the job of calculating the schedules. And lo! You will find how comfortable your body will follow the instructor. As far as sleep is concerned, both quality and quantity factors are important.

There is another point that could make a vast difference in terms of your health and longevity. Please learn to get over another Vattagenic habit, which is the restraint of natural urges of the body. Proper and timely elimination of body wastes should happen for a healthy body response. Suppressing of the natural bodily urges is in general disadvantageous, TYPE - V individuals need to take it on more serious stipulations. This is because this sort of practice makes the *vatta* dosha lose its balance.

Following are the thirteen natural urges that tend to give rise to a variety of *vatta* maladies:

Urge to urinate

This may lead to maladies like general malaise, stones in urinary tract and pain in lower abdomen.

Urge to defecate

There may be ailments like constipation and gas in abdomen, cramps in calf muscles, headache and gaseous distention of intestines and pain in abdomen.

Urge to pass the flatus

Pain in the abdomen, retention of urine and stool, exhaustion, weakened digestion and some grave diseases like loss of eye vision, heart disease and abdominal tumours may result.

Urge to burp

This may lead to loss of hunger, hiccough, bouts of cough, shivering in the body and breathlessness.

Urge to cry

Problems like running nose, headache, eye disease, dizziness, loss of appetite and heart ailments may result from this habit of suppression.

Urge to yawn

This may result in ailments like headache, weakness of the body senses and nervous system disorders like *torticollis*, tremors and numbness, facial paralysis, etc.

Urge to sleep

Habitual restraint of sleep relates to problems like heaviness in head and eyes, anxiety, lethargy and malaise. Also there may be difficulty with powers of mental concentration.

Urge to eat

Refraining from eating may cause body aches, emaciation, pain in the body, general weakness and dizziness.

Urge to drink water

Dryness of the mouth, feeling of boredom, faintness, giddiness, heart ailment and deafness may result from less or no water intake.

Urge to sneeze

Sneezing is also one of the natural instincts of the body which, when curbed, may lead to problems like headache, weakness of the sensory organs and nervous system disorders like *torticollis*, shivering of body parts, lack of sensation and facial paralysis.

Urge to vomit

When the natural urge of queasiness is subdued time and again, then this may subsequently present itself as some skin disorder like erysipelas, urticaria, skin allergies, black pigmentation of the skin and swellings. Also there may be symptoms of nausea, loss of appetite and eye ailments.

Urge to cough

Suppression of cough may be mostly circumstantial, but this practice is again *vatta* distorting. In the long run, this leads to bouts of dry cough, asthmatic attacks, tuberculosis, hiccough, anorexia and heart disease.

Urge to gasp

When there is routine holding back of fast breath due to brisk walking, exercise or any form of over-exertion, this also tends to cause *vatta* imbalance and ailments like fainting, abdominal distension and heart disease.

Urge to ejaculate

Problems like premature seminal discharge, retention of urine, pain and swelling in the reproductive organs, impotency, urinary stones and even pain in the heart region may arise due to holding onto this very urge.

V. HERBS AS HEALERS

Vatta-subsiding herbs

Ginger

Ginger is the fresh and moist rhizome of the herb called *Zingiber officinales*. It is called as *adrak* in Hindi, which means being wet. When the rhizome is dried for medicinal purposes, it is called *saunth* or *sonth*. Based on the properties by which it abides, the

Sanskrit names include *Maha-aushad* (the best medicine) and *Vishav bhaishaj* (used in a variety of ailments).

Fresh ginger is believed to be pungent in taste and the after taste is also pungent. By nature it is rough and heavy, and hot in potency. Whereas dried ginger or sounth is slimy and light and produces a sweet aftertaste.

According to Ayurvedic texts, as ginger is hot in action and heavy by nature, it helps in decreasing the aggravated *vatta* humor. The said properties of the herb also benefit the TYPE - Ks, but *pitta* personalities need to limit the intake.

In case of *vatta* imbalance, ginger may be used for hot fomentation oil to relieve TYPE - V of disorders like arthritis, gout, oedema and other forms of joint and muscle pains. For this purpose, powder of dry ginger is mixed into oil of sesame seeds or mustard oil and massaged into the joint. In a number of *vatta*-relating digestion maladies like indigestion, nausea, excessive wind formation, abdominal pain, etc., ginger comes as a great help. Also in many types of respiratory disorders like cough, cold, pneumonia, asthma, bronchitis, etc., the use of ginger is beneficial.

The ginger herb may be consumed in the form of fresh juice (5 to 10 ml) and dried ginger powder (1 to 2 g). Many Ayurvedic formulations contain it as one of the prominent ingredients.

Garlic

Garlic is a stimulant as well as rejuvenator. The properties include it being hot in action, slimy and heavy. It provides a bitter aftertaste. Garlic is gifted by nature with the five prime tastes, viz., sweet, salty, bitter, astringent and pungent, of which bitter taste is more prominent. It is carminative, a good diuretic and has a distinctive property of renewing the damaged body tissues.

Being hot and heavy by nature, the herb helps to allay *vatta* imbalance. It can be taken in a variety of ways. But garlic should be used with care in those with TYPE – P as its being hot in action could aggravate heat in the body system.

Garlic juice can be taken mixed in some quantity of boiled and cooled water. In *vatta*-related joint pains and body stiffness, the juice extracted from the herb when warmed, and massage the joint with it, provides relief from the pain as well as the swelling.

The use of garlic is also beneficial in heart ailments as it is a natural stimulant. Therefore it would be of extreme use to swallow two to three fresh bulbs daily on an empty stomach. Those suffering from high blood pressure can derive similar benefit.

Milk boiled with a few garlic bulbs is good for vigour and vitality.

Ajwain

Also known as *yavani, ajmodika and deepyika* in Sanskrit, ajwain is light, rough and robust in nature. The taste is bitter and pungent and the aftertaste is bitter. It is hot in potency. Thus the herb helps alleviate *vatta* (and also *kapha*) but might cause an increase in the fire humor.

In many forms of abdominal distress relating to *vatta* aggravation, be it indigestion, loss of appetite, bloating, excessive wind formation, nausea and vomiting, abdominal distention, pain in the abdomen, etc., ajwain provides relief.

Ajwain is also the possessor of some unique anti-toxic properties. According to Ayurvedic texts, the use of the herb is also good for the heart. In disorders like weakness of the heart, ajwain being hot, is stimulating in action. Another specific effect of ajwain is that it combats fever and at the same time it provides warmth to the body. Thus the use of the same has been signified in fever along with shivering. *Vatta* individuals may include this herb in everyday meals or therapeutically 1 to 3 grams of the powder of ajwain may be taken along with warm water.

As for the herb of the benefits in *kapha* imbalance, ailments like chronic cough associated with excessive formation of phlegm (productive cough) and also when there is bad smell due to the persistent phlegm or in bronchial asthma, when phlegm remains stuck in the bronchioles, ajwain helps to subside the excessive production of phlegm.

Large Cardamom

Large cardamom is light and rough by nature and hot in potency. The *rasas* or tastes are bitter and pungent, whereas the after-taste is bitter. Being bitter and hot, *badi elaychi* causes a decrease in the air and phlegm humors of the body. At the same time it tends to increase the heat or '*pitta*'.

Vatta naturally intrudes digestion and the imbalance may cause a number of digestion maladies like loss of appetite, indigestion, dyspepsia, occasional nausea, feeling of discomfort after a meal, excessive thirst, excessive wind formation and stomach ache, etc., which can be relieved by taking the large cardamom. The seeds of the herb are to be pounded and the powder is to be taken in a dose of 1 to 3 grams approximately, preferably with some warm water.

In case of fever of different types when there are chills and rigours along with the rise in temperature, the large cardamom again proves useful. It is advisable to take the recommended dose of powder of the seeds along with lukewarm water twice in a day's time. The herb is also believed to be a holder of anti-toxic and anti-infective properties and its use could help combat an underlying infection.

As specified earlier, the large cardamom also combats phlegm. In case of recurrent bouts of cold and cough, try taking the herb in the form of a powder or a decoction of the same. For better results add some honey to it. When there is headache in addition to the nasal congestion, you could also add some powdered cardamom to the balm or oil and massage the forehead with it.

2 TYPE – P Personality (The *pitta* type)

TYPE – P is the fire personality with the natural traits of the fire element.

I. SELF-IDENTIFICATION

The basic properties of the fire humor reflect in a *pitta* personality.

1. *Ushna* – hot. The *pitta* person is bound be hot-tempered. Also the body temperature remains on warmer side making external cool more amiable.
2. *Tikshana* – sharp. He has a sharp intellect and the body features may also concur with this quality.
3. *Drava* – flowing, fluid. This causes more perspiration and also assertive nature.
4. *Sara* – mobile. This individual remains on the go with busy schedules.
5. *Snigdha* – oily, viscous. Skin and hair would have oily texture and radiance.

The mental state of *satwa guna* makes the TYPE – P to be more knowledgeable, logical and worldly wise.

1. He is a holder of smooth skin with yellowish or reddish

tinge. Soles of the feet, palms, lips and tongue are more red-coloured than other body parts.

2. Often, skin afflictions like pimples and acne, freckles, moles and birthmarks are common skin afflictions.
3. Generally intolerant to heat.
4. There is sparse and slow hair growth and the hair show signs of premature greying.
5. He gives importance to the daily diet intake and is a good eater. Also, tends to show preference towards cold and chilled food items.
6. Perspiration is profuse, finds it difficult to bear high temperatures and shows liking towards use of perfumes, scented talcs, deodorants, etc.
7. There is tendency to feel exhausted easily but has moderate or optimum resistance power.
8. Moderate sexual desire and limited popularity among the opposite sex.
9. Losing temper over small issues is common. And remain fearless and vigorous in any situation when he feels opposed.
10. TYPE – P is possessor of great mental powers of intelligence, retentive memory and logical understanding (owing to the *satvic* mental state of manifestation). Decision-making is not a tough deal for the *pitta* person.
11. Dreams are more of fire, flame, lightening, flashes, meteors and red-coloured flowers.

In this type, the *pitta* dosha is found to be predominant. Therefore, the nature of an individual possessing this particular prakriti type will show most of the properties of the fire body humor like heat, sharpness, flowing, mobility and being viscous.

This type of nature is moderately balanced and focussed. The individual, overall, leads a healthy life full of vigour.

The body of an individual with TYPE – P of prakriti is generally symmetrical and pleasant-looking. The complexion is fair. The nails, hands, feet, eye and face show a tinge of copper colour. Eyes are generally small and eyelashes are less dense. Hair growth on his body is less. The hair loses colour early in life or he might go bald. He perspires a lot and his perspiration gives foul odour. His skin is more likely to show moles, pimples and blemishes. This type of person feels more hungry and thirsty as compared to normal people. Due to the hot nature of *pitta*, the person cannot bear heat and finds relief in cold climates. The body temperature remains towards warmer side.

Basic temperament

By nature, this person is fast and active. He gets angry very soon and soon gets calmed. He is fond of dressing up and looking good. He shows qualities of being courageous, heroic in deeds, bears good intellect and possesses wonderful power of memory. He has a good moral character but easily gets envious and reacts accordingly. It is believed that a person with *pitta* prakriti shows mental temperaments of *satwa* mind. Owing to this, he does not feel pompous during periods of contentment and adverse conditions would not make him grieve. The *satwa* aspect keeps the mental balance. The dreams of TYPE – P of individual are more of fire, sun, volcanoes, lightning, etc.

II. SELF-UNDERSTANDING

Imbalance in TYPE – P

Naturally, the *pitta* or fire humor is aggravated in the middle age, in the middle period of the day, i.e. afternoons and middle part of night, while taking meals and in autumn season.

The diet imbalance in TYPE – P

In diet, taking in more of food items that are sour, salty and pungent in taste aggravates the fire.

The fire humor may be thrown out of balance by frequent intake of hot foods and beverages, chillies, fried foods and spices. And also hard drinks and alcoholic or fermented drinks would imbalance the dosha in TYPE - P individuals.

The lifestyle imbalance in TYPE - P

1. Over-indulgence in sex.
2. Excessive anger and episodes of jealousy and high expectations, and also fretting over nominal issues.

Similarities in the fire humor with diet and daily activities having similar traits would cause the same to get aggravated and imbalanced.

1. *Ushna* – hot. Taking foods with hot potency and staying in fairly warm environment for a long time.
2. *Tikshana* – sharp. Severe reaction to *pitta* emotions and also taking of intense, spicy and potent diet.
3. *Drava* – flowing. Remaining emotionally intense and always on the run.
4. *Sara* – mobile. Keeping superfluous busy schedules with no or very little physical and mental respite.
5. *Snigdha* – oily, viscous. Intake of oily and fried foods.

The mental state of *satwa guna* is predominant in *pitta* which makes the fire person highly intellectual. Yet, imbalance draws in when the mental positive virtues are overpowered by *pitta* emotions of criticism, over judgment and antagonism.

Signs of imbalance in TYPE - P

When the fire humor aggravates, it is likely to present the signs that are similar to its properties. *Pitta* discrepancy can be perceived by some basic signs like:

1. There is burning sensation in the body.
2. Vertigo and superfluous tiredness could be astounding.
3. There might be acidic eructation and bitter taste in the mouth.
4. There is yellowing of eyes, urine and skin.
5. Natural liking for cool stuffs is also indicative.
6. Mental attributes of failure of demarcation between right wrong may take the form of uncertainty.
7. Episodes of unconditional disapproval and irritation prevail.
8. The *pitta* imbalance person may show signs of becoming jealous, critical and over-condemnatory. Mainly the mental imbalance in TYPE - P person would be the failure of discrimination.

Forty ailments that may be encountered by TYPE – P

1. *Osa* – Heat stroke
2. *Plosa* – Scorching of the skin
3. *Daha* – Burning of the skin
4. *Dawathu* – Burning sensation in sense organs like eyes, etc.
5. *Dhumaka* – Feeling of fumes coming out from the head.
6. *Analaka* – Acid eructation.
7. *Vidaha* – Burning sensation in the palms, soles of the feet
8. *Antardaha* – Burning sensation in the entire body
9. *Amsadaha* – Burning sensation in a part of the body
10. *Ushmadhikaya* – Very high body temperature
11. *Atisweda* – Excessive perspiration
12. *Angasweda* – Sweating of a part of the body
13. *Angagandha* – Body odour
14. *Anga vardhna* – Fissures on the surface of the body
15. *Shonitakleda* – Pernicious anemia
16. *Mamsakleda* – Degeneration and softening of the muscular tissues

17. *Twagdaha* - Burning sensation in the skin
18. *Mamsadaha* - Burning sensation in the muscles
19. *Twagavadarana* - Cracking or scaling of the skin
20. *Charmavadarana* - Deep cracking of the skin
21. *Raktakotha* - Putrefaction of the blood
22. *Rakta-pitta* - Bleeding from body pores
23. *Haritatwa* - Greenish colour of the skin
24. *Nilika* - Blue moles
25. *Kaksha* - Herpes
26. *Kamala* - Jaundice
27. *Raktamandala* - Red wheels on the skin
28. *Haridratva* - Yellowish colour
29. *Tiktasyata* - Bitter taste of the mouth
30. *Putimukhata* - Offensive smell from the mouth
31. *Trishnadhikya* - Excessive thirst
32. *Atripti* - Unsatisfied hunger
33. *Ashyapak* - Mouth ulcers
34. *Galapaka* - Inflammation of the throat
35. *Akshipaka* - Conjunctivitis
36. *Gudapaka* - Proctitis of the anal region
37. *Medhrapaka* - Inflammation of the penis
38. *Jivadana* - Haemorrhage
39. *Tamahpravesa* - Unconsciousness, fainting
40. *Haritharida netra, mootra varchastva* - Greenish and yellowish colouration of the eyes, urine and faeces.

III. SELF CARE

Lifestyle changes for the TYPE – P

To combat *pitta* imbalance, it is recommended to take up the regime that renders opposing qualities as that of the fire humor. In case you are TYPE – P, simply recall the fire traits that are rather dominant within you and try to subsist with just the contrary. Let us now revise all the traits that direct a fire person.

1. *Ushna* – hot. Going against this characteristic, cool and calming foodstuff and cold drinks would prove to be relieving. It is also suggested that a TYPE - P individual spends most of his time in a colder environment.
2. *Tikshana* – sharp. Maintaining easy-going attitude and evading potent and intense foods is needed.
3. *Drava* – flowing, fluid. All stressful conditions and nervous tension needs to be avoided. One should also practise more to tame anger.
4. *Sara* – mobile. Mobility needs to be hampered. Quite the reverse, physical and mental rest is needed.
5. *Snigdha* – oily, viscous. As you already have more of fire in your system, fried and unctuous diet needs to be restricted. Also any application of oils on body may be replaced by soothing cremes.

The mental state of *satwa guna* is predominant in *pitta*. This virtue may be easily maintained by the TYPE - P by incorporating positive mental traits of being logical, decisive and ambitious.

According to Ayurveda text, just as in tradition one treats a son-in-law (especially in India) with paramount care and respect, and serves him sweetened cold drinks and comforting foods, a TYPE - P individual should take similar special care of himself.

Pitam jamatramiva madhur sheetalayajayate

Earlier, it was stated that a TYPE - V individual needs to stick to timetables so as to keep his dosha balanced. But this lifestyle would rather invalidate the fire types. TYPE - P people need to go easy with their schedules. As *pitta* timing is already at all times perfect and scheduled, it makes sense to de-organise at times.

Now let us understand the problem with TYPE – P people that flings them out of equilibrium. *Pitta* or the fire is in itself highly organised and demanding, and hence this makes the TYPE – P individuals exceedingly critical both of themselves and the ambience. They tend to get worked up over every little thing that seems out of order, and unintentionally time and again intensifies the fire within their system. A relaxed and compassionate attitude towards themselves and the world is the perquisite need of such type of individuals.

Diet management in TYPE – P

As diet is one of the most essential preconditions for survival, food contemplation for the TYPE – P is rather indispensable. As the gastric fire is vigorous, digestion would be markedly good. Therefore, a *pitta* person needs to snack more often (to avoid gastric burning and hypoglycemia).The low sugar levels due to easy combustion of food would further cause undue irritation and weakness. The three tastes that have been optional are sweet, bitter and astringent. More sweets, succulent fruits, sweetened desserts and fruit juices (that would be banned for the *kapha* person) are rather recommended for the fire types.

As oil is to *vatta*, and honey is for *kapha*, *ghee* is to *pitta*. A TYPE – P person needs to avoid intake of oils and yet feast on ghee, more so on ghee prepared with cooling and calming herbs. Even massage with ghee is recommended. Milk and milk products are another dietary boon for TYPE – P individual.

Lifestyle management in TYPE – P

As the property of the fire humor is hot and intense, Ayurveda suggests living in cooler, soothing and calming environment, away from sweating and parching heat. The imbalance could only be refined by imbibing whatever is cooling and soothing. Cold tub-bath and using soft, cooling, fragrant herbs like sandalwood, camphor, *khas khas* and rose in the form of body pastes is beneficial.

Bathing and swimming in cool and fragrant water would be soothing for *pitta* aggravation. Enjoying purposefully, and more often listening to amiable and relaxing, pleasant music would be beneficial.

Some activities like cuddling and rejoicing with kids and beautiful women have been advocated as it has a lasting soothing effect on the mind.

Massage is also good for TYPE – P personalities, but the choice of oil should be a cooling one like coconut, or even better, fragrant and soothing and calming crèmes should be applied.

Let us now talk about *pitta* relaxation. Sleep of a TYPE – P person can be easily affected by external stimuli like lights, sound, etc. If you are this kind of personality, then you would need to keep your room dark and mildly scented with rose petals, lavender oil drops or henna leaves, so as to ensure yourself a sound sleep that calms your strained nerves. Having a nap in the moonlight or amidst cool air and showers, or in cool dark shade will do you good. To top it all, Ayurveda suggests the TYPE – P person should wear ornaments such as necklaces made of fragrant sandalwood, lotus or pearls and listen to soft melodies. All this would help him relax physically and mentally and help reduce the intensified fire within.

Possessing the virtue of being sharp in intellect and memory may at times hamper the mental balance and aggravate *pitta*. Therefore the individual needs to incorporate necessary periodic holidays for himself, and also a simple hobby (that is not challenging) may be brought into practice.

Also, so as to keep the mental cool, spending leisure time with friends and loved ones is desirable. Listening to soothing musical melodies or else sweet words of a devoted one could be actually relieving.

Out of the five senses, the sense of sight relates to *pitta* humor.

Thus visual effects leave lasting impression on the fire types. Rejoicing and relaxing in scenic surroundings would surely have a serene effect on the mind.

Subtle meditation and *Bhramari Pranayaam* is advisable to help alleviate the distorted fire. In fact all breathing exercises when commenced with left nostril, leave an overall cooling effect. And this is required for the *pitta* person. During meditation, the *pitta* person may concentrate on the flame of a *diya* (preferably burning in ghee) or candle, as per the image effect. All other forms of exercise need to be practised moderately or before self-challenging situations arise. *Pitta* lifestyle and diet is analogous to the ones advocated in summers. Or in summers we should lead a life like a *pitta* person.

As for panchkarma treatment in Ayurveda, *virechan karma* or inducting purgatives is the best possible therapy for subsiding and imbalanced fire humor. The therapy of *virechana* (inducing purgation) and use of ghee and also use of milk (both externally and internally) has been suggested so as to calm the exacerbated *pitta*.

IV. SELF-HELP GUIDE FOR TYPE – P

Diet

TYPE – P individuals are born with a good BMR (Basal Metabolic Rate). So in case you fall in this category, you need to munch every two hours. This would help to keep your blood glucose levels intact and give you fewer chances to wither. Also, as you generally have invigorated gastric fire, snacking more often is permissible to you, only you need to be conscious about the right choice.

Tastes

Out of the six basic tastes, viz., sweet, salty, sour, pungent, bitter and astringent, there are three tastes that are recommended for TYPE – P people and these are sweet, bitter and astringent. The rest three tastes of salty, sour and pungent need to be restricted in daily diet.

Herbs

There are some kitchen herbs that tend to alleviate body heat owing to the basic property these herbs hold. This includes the herbs that generally have traits like being cooling and soothing, with taste by and large sweet, and astringent or bitter, and the after-taste is mostly sweet.

Please refer to the four main *pitta*-alleviating herbs, namely, fennel, liquorice, cardamom and aloe vera that have been detailed further in the book. Also you may go through the Herbs as Healers index in the second part of the book to know more. Other than the four herbs, TYPE - P individuals may balance their fire dosha with the use of cumin, peppermint, rose, saffron, sandalwood, coriander, asparagus, etc.

Condiments

TYPE - P person has to be rather choosy with his intake of condiments and spices as mostly these aggravate the fire. A few spices like cardamoms, fennel, cloves, coriander and black pepper (in less quantity) are suitable for the fire person.

Vegetables

As a *pitta* person, you may feast on most vegetables with sweet, bitter and astringent tastes, and remember to avoid pungent and sour ones. Carrot, spinach, asparagus, cucumber, cabbage, beans, peas, bottle gourd, bitter gourd, white gourd, potatoes, sweet potatoes and broccoli may all be taken.

Fruits

Fruits are meant for you as all juicy, sweet and astringent and also dry fruits would mostly do no harm. Melons, water melon, grapes (not sour), papaya, apples, apricot, ripe mango (in moderation), bananas, coconut, lichi, resins, figs, sugarcane, etc., are acceptable. Restrict your intake of sour fruits like tamarind, berries, lime, orange (sour) and pineapple. Fruit juice when naturally sweet are also advocated for you.

Restricted diet

Spicy, fried, sour foods, and hot and potent diet like spicy soups, tea and coffee are not really advocated for the *pitta* types. Foods like green and red chilies, ginger, garlic and most of the spices need to be used sparsely.

Fasting for TYPE – P

For the TYPE – P personalities who have intense fire in their system, fasting completely on water can never be advised. As it is they have a high metabolic rate and if they are made to avoid food completely, this may harm their body tissues. Therefore, if they have to go on fast, they should never try to prolong it lest it intervenes with their comfort level. They need not be strict with themselves. Fruit intake as raw or as fresh juice should be inculcated. The juice may be diluted with water so as to derive better results from fasting. Vegetable salad, vegetable juice or bland vegetable soup without any spices can also be taken. Or in case more is needed then mono diet fasts (where only one kind of food is taken the whole day) can be kept.

Essential oils

Lavender oil and rose oil are particularly cooling, calming and relaxing and therefore may be used in the room for pleasant aroma, or gently rubbed on skin during bath to increase the effect. Sandalwood oil may be used for gently massaging the forehead just before sleeping.

Sleep pattern

Mind and body relaxation is highly desirable for those with *pitta* type personality. The reason being that by nature you over-work.

You do not need scheduling like *vatta* personalities, yet more often try to unwind and soothe your strained nerves. As much as seven to eight hours of sleep is vital for you; you normally get disturbed easily. You are sensitive to light; make sure that there is complete darkness in the room when you take a nap. Rubbing coconut oil on the soles of your feet, burning lavender oil in perfume sticks and scattering a few rose petals or juvenile leaves of henna on your pillow would assure you a goodnight's sleep. Being overtly sexually active would leave you both mentally and physically exhausted. In that case you need to replenish with some natural aphrodisiacs.

Exercise and Yoga for TYPE – P

Some of the suggested yoga asanas are:

1. *Dhanurasana*
2. *Bhujang Asana*
3. *Ardha matsyendra Asana*
4. *Shalabh Asana*
5. *Trikon Asana*
6. *Paschimottan Asana*
7. *Makarasana*
8. *Shava Asana*

Some *pranayaam* or breathing techniques for TYPE – P

1. *Chander bhedi Pranayaam*
2. *Bhramari Pranayaam*
3. *Sheetali*
4. *Shitkari*

Mudra or hand alignment for TYPE – P

1. *Dhyan Mudra*
2. *Gyana Mudra*
3. *Prana Mudra*
4. *Varuna Mudra*

Other highly beneficial yoga *kriyas* or methods for TYPE – P

1. *Kunjal Kriya*
2. *Sutra Neti* in milk

Massage therapy

As a *pitta* person, you need to incorporate soothing and relaxing movements during massage. You should use oils which give cooling effect. Creams with soothing fragrance or coconut oil would do the trick. It would be all the more effective if herb powder of sandalwood or lesser cardamom or even camphor is added to the same. During massage you need feather touch, gentle rubbing and wringing strokes.

Colour therapy

Being a TYPE – P person, you need to avoid the use of dark, bright and warming shades of red, orange, black, etc. Rather you need to integrate soothing and calming colours of green, white and blue. You may use these colours frequently in your room linen, in your dresses and dress accessories. Particularly sun-charged water with cool shades of blue and purple can be taken. Although, while dealing with colours you should keep this in mind that dark violet colour may sometimes cause congestion. At the same time glycerine charged with blue colour may be used by *pitta* persons to combat the fire maladies like mouth ulcers and burning sensation.

Gem therapy

Gem stones in rings, bracelet or necklace can be opted for. For better results, one should make sure that the gems are in direct contact with the skin. Diamond, pearl and the blue sapphire are some gems that have a cooling effect and are thus suitable for *pitta* people.

Meditation

Meditation is a sure boon for the TYPE – P as it has rejuvenation effect on both, body and soul. It is, therefore, required to free the mind of all work-related worries and other worldly thoughts. Detachment is not only a boon, but one of the most inevitable features of our basic personality. And let me emphasise that everyday practice of this sort will reward you with peace and tranquillity (which you need more than the other two persona types) throughout your life. Now as the sense of sight is the most relative source that connects to your being, yoga therapy of *Trataka* would be of great help in this practice. For the same you may daze onto the flame of a burning candle or simply visualise some meditation motif like *Omkara* or even the image of God.

Chakra balance

TYPE – P person needs to focus on the Manipurak Chakra. This is situated at the umbilicus and is yellow in colour. During meditation you need to envisage this yellow chakra. This brings inner relaxation and serenity.

Seasonal support

You may find more ailments generating due to dominance of *pitta* or fire humor in the body particularly during the autumn season. This happens because there is natural aggravation of *pitta* during this season. It is during the rains that this dosha gets accumulated in the body system. For this reason, there is acidic reaction of food as the plants and water become turbid during this period of the year. Early winter is the time or season when this humor shows signs of mitigation all by itself.

Suggested hobbies and career

You can develop hobbies like reading, gardening, painting, listening to music and sightseeing in the lap of nature. Watching beautiful scenery acts as food to your sense of sight. You can take up some sports activity (as you are not short of stamina) but remember never to become competitive and overdo the activity. Even long walks in cool shade of the trees or during the wee hours of the morning would suit you. You need to plan for more relaxing holidays when your work schedule evades you both physically and mentally. As for the choice of your career, try to opt for what suits your intellect, concern, efficiency and at the same time keeps you on the driver's seat (you do not like to be driven). TYPE – P individual is blessed with *satwa guna* of the mind and so you need to be convinced whenever you are deciding for yourself. Professions like financial consultancy, corporate executives, professors or researchers will be fine for you.

Moreover, all rational and intellectual activities would be all the more result-prone when practised during the *pitta* intellect time, i.e. preferably between 10 a.m. and 2 p.m.

Important norms

The best suggested norm for a *pitta* person or the TYPE – P individual would be to relax and try to be as less judgmental as possible.

V. HERBS AS HEALERS

Pitta-subsiding herbs

Fennel

One among a number of kitchen ingredients in daily use fennel or *saunf* is sweet, bitter and pungent in taste and the after-taste is refreshingly sweet. Light and rough by nature, it is cold in action. Therefore, fennel decreases the fire humor in the body and thus finds use in treating a number of related ailments.

Fennel can be roasted and powdered. You can take this powder in case of abdominal discomfort or stomach ache. In case of habitual constipation, try taking it with warm milk at bedtime.

In case of nausea or vomiting which may result from *pitta* imbalance, equal quantities of powdered fennel and dried mint leaves may be boiled in water till one-fourth remains. This decoction can be taken 3 to 4 times in a day.

Another of *pitta* manifestation is ulcer formation in the body. Gastric ulcers may benefit by regular intake of this herb. Also so as to relieve mouth ulcers, approximately two teaspoons of fennel may be boiled in a glassful of water. After it gets cooled down, a piece of roasted alum is to be added to the same. This can be used for gargles.

In case the excessive fire humor causes skin afflictions with burning sensation and itching, burning of hands and feet, recurrent boils, etc., then a powder may be prepared with equal parts of fennel and dry coriander. To the same double the quantity of powdered *mishri* is to be added. This powder can be taken twice daily for some days in a dose of 3 to 5 grams approximately. For children the dose would be half.

Licorice

Roots of the plant called Liquorice or *Yashtimadhu* (Latin *Glycyrrhiza glabra*) better known by the name *mulathee*, are sweet in taste. They also leave a sweet after-taste. By nature it is heavy and slimy and cold in action.

According to Ayurvedic texts, as the herb is sweet in taste and cold in action, it helps bringing down the increased *pitta* or heat in the body. Mulathee being heavy, slimy and sweet helps in decreasing the aggravated *vatta* or air body humor. Therefore, it is helpful in treating the diseases relating to vitiation in air and fire body humors.

Liquorice is yellowish and fibrous from inside and contains a peculiarly pleasant smell and a distinctive flavour. For ages, it has been used as a household remedy for treating the maladies of cough and colds. This owes to the property of mulathee of melting and extracting phlegm. Other than this, it has proved useful widely in a number of other ailments. Used as a mild purgative, it also acts as blood purifier. It is good for the voice, eyes and hair.

Liquorice not only increases the stamina and fertility, it is also useful in the problems of excessive thirst, toxicity and nausea. As a medicine it is used for curing the disorders like scabies, rickets, headaches, anemia and urinary infections. Liquorice also acts as an aphrodisiac and is said to keep away premature aging.

About 3 to 5 grams of the powdered mulathee when taken along with cow's milk is a good cure for acidity and heals stomach ulcers.

Liquorice has been found fairly handy in treating dry cough. One teaspoon of the powder of the same mixed with honey may be taken once or twice a day. It even benefits chronic coughs or coughs accompanied by blood.

A decoction prepared from liquorice can be gargled as well as swallowed. This is a remedy for not only mouth ulcers due to excessive *pitta*, but also is good for pain in the throat and inflammation of the vocal cords.

Cardamom

Cardamom is light and rough in nature and cold in potency. The taste is sweet and bitter, while the after-taste is sweet. It is one of the rare herbs that are gifted with the property to destroy an aggravation in all the three humors of the body, viz., air, fire and phlegm. Therefore cardamom cures a large number of ailments. The taste and after-taste being sweet and the herb being cold in nature, it is beneficial in the *pitta* imbalance. The lesser cardamom is a good digestive. It is advisable to slowly chew one or two of it after a meal. This would not only help you with easy assimilation of food, but also act as a mouth freshener. Its regular habit also ensures a better appetite and inclination for the food.

Being soothing and calming by nature and cold in action, cardamom tends to relieve body heat and can be taken to curb any sort of burning sensation in the body. It may be a burning in the stomach, mouth, soles of the feet and hands, a burning perception in the eyes or burning urination. The recommended dosage of cardamom powder is approximately half to one gram. It can be taken along with water or milk twice a day.

Sometimes when there is a vomiting sensation, chewing of one or two cardamoms and slowly swallowing the juice of the herb helps combat the distress. Also, a decoction may be prepared by boiling cardamom along with some mint leaves. This can be taken with some mishri added to it in small quantities at regular intervals. In the case of children, cardamom may be pounded and the kids are made to lick the same mixed with a little honey.

Aloe vera

Aloe vera or *ghritkumari* as the local Hindi name of the herb is, is recommended for curing *pitta* imbalance. The small 1 to 2 feet long herb, having big and fleshy leaves with mildly thorny outline is easy to find.

Aloe vera is also regarded as a *rasayana*, i.e. that which strengthens the immune system of the body and keeps diseases at bay. This herb is slimy and mucoid by nature, and cold in action. All these traits of the herb make it beneficial for relieving fire aggravation. Also, it is bitter in taste and leaves a pungent after-taste. Therefore it is acceptable for TYPE – Ks.

The herb may be used both internally as well as for local application. The usage is plenty.

Pulp extracted from the leaves of the herb can be taken on an empty stomach first time in the morning. The fresh juice when taken in a dose of 10 to 20 ml two or three times a day is a good cure for relieving maladies like hyperacidity and burning sensation. In case of burns and scalds, the juice extracted from the pulp applied on the burned area is both a soother and healer.

Having the property of soothing and calming the body system by means of alleviating body heat, it is also beneficial in healing wounds, oedema, pain, inflammation and other skin diseases.

As for local application for pain and swelling in body parts, some turmeric powder may be mixed into the pulp of aloe vera and this has to be heated on fire and applied to the affected part for relief.

Pitta debility generally owing to excessive heat and use of energy in the system can be relieved by another home remedy using this herb. Hundred grams of the pulp and one kilogram milk are to be mixed together and heated on low fire. This is to be taken twice a day with sugar added to the same in a dose of one tablespoon.

3 TYPE – K Personality (The *kapha* type)

You may discover yourself as TYPE – K individual when you find yourself being deliberately slow and steady, and at times rather sluggish, which are the basic traits of the *kapha* dosha.

I. SELF-IDENTIFICATION

All the properties of *kapha* humor come obvious in its persona type.

1. *Guru* – heavy. The individual is heavy-boned with bodily frame on the heavier side.
2. *Snigdha* – oily, viscous. Skin and hair are more oily and supple.
3. *Pichhila* – turbid, gelatinous. This accounts for the slow pace of both body and mind.
4. *Shita* – cold, cooling. Skin is cool and environmental warmth is much needed.
5. *Sthula* – coarse. He tends to put on weight effortlessly.
6. *Sthira* – stable, motionless. This person has slow body movements and thinking is unwavering.
7. *Slakshma* – smooth. *Kapha* person has smooth skin and exhibits slow, steady and even poise.

The mental state of *tamas guna* predominates in this particular humor. This makes this individual remain attached and also sometimes avaricious.

1. A person with phlegm as dominant humor is a holder of symmetrical and proportionate body and a good stable physique emitting the aura of endurance, strength and stability. The muscles and tissues of his body are well developed.
2. Tends to gain weight more easily.
3. The skin is soft, smooth, supple and particularly greasy and glowing. It generally feels cool and gives bluish radiance. Also, the hair texture is slightly greasy but thick, maybe curly and distinctively dark-coloured.
4. He tends to be a slow and calm eater and thus normally stays clear of digestive afflictions, although digestion of a *kapha* person is apparently slow.
5. Particularly fond of sweet food items.
6. Remains calm and steady, and does not get excited or irritated easily.
7. Also, although the intelligence levels are well developed, he takes more time in coming to conclusions. Holds high morals of respect, trust, equality and has an overall giving nature.
8. He has particularly good capacity to tolerate pain and fatigue, and does not tend to complain easily.
9. Possessor of pleasant voice with a deep pitch. The voice can be compared to the roaring of a lion, beating of a drum or rambling of a cloud.
10. *Kapha* dreams may more often pertain to waterfalls, large lakes, swans, clouds, flowers and birds.

The individual who bears dominance of *kapha* dosha shows

similar characteristics as the properties of this body humor, i.e. coldness, heaviness, viscous, motionless, soft, sliminess and turbidity.

This prakriti type is however considered to be the best among all the three types and the individual possessing it enjoys a long and stable life with less incidence of illness. The body of the individuals having phlegm as the dominant humor is generally well built, symmetrical and beautiful. All the body parts are stable and look healthy and full. The complexion is normally fair, rosy, like a lotus and with the glow of golden colour. His eyes are large, shiny and reveal happiness. Hair on the body is black and shining. The *kapha* individual begets a hefty appearance and is an easy gainer of unwanted pounds. The individual with *kapha* prakriti has a stable and steady walk. He works with patience and calm. He is never in a hurry owing to the slow nature of the *kapha*. His voice is strong like the depth of the sea or a lion. He is fertile and leads a healthy life span with less occurrence of disease.

Basic temperament

This person is pious, prudish, truthful and grateful by nature and bears a fine moral character. He has a reasonably fine memory. He has a stable nature, does not change his mind very often and is not impulsive. By nature this person is patient, respectful, not easily affected by adverse conditions, courageous, free from greed and jealousy, and is affluent and courteous. He thinks about pros and cons before performing any action, and makes decisions with wisdom. He can patiently forego the adverse conditions like grief, violence, hunger and thirst. The person does not get angry or grieved very easily. His main temperament is of tamas-mental category. The TYPE – K person would naturally not get excited in happiness and would not grieve during unhappy times but would show patience, modesty and calmness in both states. But at times by virtue of *tamas guna*, as a *kapha* persona, he would tend to hold on to grief and anguish. The attribute of *tamas* may make him very possessive and attached. It could even make the person highly sedentary, inert and dormant.

II. SELF-UNDERSTANDING

Imbalance in TYPE – K

The *kapha* dosha is believed to show natural aggravation in the younger age, during early mornings, during the start of a meal, during snowfall and in the spring season.

The diet imbalance in TYPE – K

Foods that are more cold, heavy and unctuous, and increased intake of sweets or foodstuffs that are sweet in taste, milk and milk products would cause easy aggravation of *kapha* in TYPE – K individuals. Of the six basic tastes known to human tongue, the phlegm humor tends to exacerbate by more intake of sweet, salty and sour tastes.

The lifestyle imbalance in TYPE – K

1. Sleeping during daytime.
2. Keeping a relaxed and carefree attitude and taking in less stress and strain in day-to-day activities.
3. Less mental exertion.
4. Less or no exercise routine.
5. Also, less physical and vocal activity and leading a lethargic and sedentary lifestyle.

Likeness between the *kapha* dosha and the everyday routine (diet and lifestyle) of TYPE – K personality tends to aggravate the same and causes imbalance.

1. *Guru* – heavy. Taking in of heavy diet or overeating.
2. *Snigdha* – oily, viscous. Fried, oily and unctuous foods.
3. *Pichhila* – turbid, gelatinous. All slimy, viscous foods and beverages.
4. *Shita* – cold, cooling. Cold environment and cold foods

and drinks like soft drinks, sweetened beverages and ice creams.

5. *Sthula* – coarse. The tendency of TYPE – K personality to hold on to fixations and emotions does more harm by eventually throwing *kapha* out of kelter.
6. *Sthira* – stable, motionless. Leading sedentary life, sitting or resting for too long and especially sleeping during day time causes imbalance.
7. *Slakshma* – smooth. Using smooth textures, living easy, carefree attitude in daily routine.

The mental state of *tamas guna* predominates in this particular personality. When this takes the form of negative mental emotions like possessiveness and acquisitiveness, *kapha* plunges out of balance.

Signs of imbalance in TYPE – K

Kapha aggravation or imbalance would show some peculiar indications like:

1. There is feeling of heaviness and stiffness in the body.
2. Weight gain, plumpness and swelling in body parts comes easily.
3. Skin and hair are oilier than normal.
4. Prolonged sweet taste in mouth and occasional sensation of nausea.
5. There may be excessive sleep or lethargy.
6. Excessive phlegm formation, especially during the early mornings.
7. Sinuses and the entire respiratory system are easily affected.
8. Morning time congestion, heaviness and lethargy is noticeable.

On psychological matters, emotions of possessiveness and overattachment are apparent. Incapability of willpower sets in making the *kapha* person all the more dormant and inert. Sometimes *kapha* imbalance might promote greed and acquisitiveness.

Mental imbalance in TYPE – K personage is the fear of determination.

Twenty ailments may be encountered by TYPE – K

1. *Tripti* – Feeling of full abdomen
2. *Tandra* – Drowsiness
3. *Nidradhikya* – Excessive sleep
4. *Staimitya* – Feeling of wet cloth covering the body
5. *Gurugatrata* – Heaviness of the body
6. *Aalasya* – Feeling of lethargy
7. *Mukhamadhuraya* – Sweet taste in the mouth
8. *Mukhasrava* – Excessive salivation from the mouth
9. *Shleshmodgirana* – Mucous expectoration
10. *Malashyadhikya* – Excessive formation of faecal wastes
11. *Kathopalepa* – Excessive mucous production in the throat
12. *Balashaka* – Tiredness, loss of strength
13. *Hridayoplepa* – Feeling of wet cloth tied to heart region
14. *Dhamanipratichaya* – Thickening or dilation of the blood vessels
15. *Galaganda* – Goitre, tumour in the neck
16. *Atisthaulya* – Obesity
17. *Sitagnita* – Suppression of digestion
18. *Udarda* – Urticaria
19. *Shwetava bhasata* – Paleness of the skin
20. *Shwetamutra netra varchastva* – Whitish colour of the eyes, urine and faeces

III. SELF CARE

Kapha imbalance needs strict guidelines for self handling. This is because the *kapha* individual has a propensity to be more rigid and stubborn with his likes and tastes.

All the similarities between the phlegm humor and the routines (diet and lifestyle) tend to aggravate the same in the TYPE - K personalities. Consequently, just like in other humor types, you need to go against the basic properties of *kapha*.

1. *Guru* – heavy. Avoidance of overeating and heavy foods and on the contrary, intake of intense and potent diet is needed.
2. *Snigdha* – oily, viscous. Fried and oily foods are to be discouraged in diet. Also to avoid oil, even the external application of oils on the body may be replaced with dry massages.
3. *Pichhila* – turbid, gelatinous. Intake of thick and slimy foodstuffs needs to be restricted.
4. *Shita* – cold, cooling. Environmental cold could be replaced by moving on to warmer surroundings and taking in of warm diet is comforting.
5. *Sthula* – coarse. Taking less diet and periodical fasting is beneficial.
6. *Sthira* – stable, motionless. Vigorous workouts, avoidance of afternoon naps and practising mental exercise is needed. Also more of talking and involvement in manual activities would do good.
7. *Slakshma* – smooth. Using coarse cloth textures and more often taking up strenuous tasks spontaneously and voluntarily proves beneficial.

As per the mental trait existing in TYPE - K, it has been stated earlier that the mental state of *tamas guna* naturally dominates *kapha*. In case you experience more of *kapha* within you, it is suggested that you try to improvise and integrate positive emotions like harmony, empathy and caring. This could keep the abysmal of *tamas guna* away.

Ayurveda suggests that a *kapha* type individual can do good only to himself if he treats himself just like he would treat his enemy.

Kapham durjanava tikshanaya

In other words, TYPE – K needs to be harsh and strict with himself, as in truth this individual remains largely self-pampered (contrary to TYPE – P).

The stubborn *kapha* is rather tricky to treat. This is mainly because of the inert trait of the earth element that this humor imbibes. Hence all intricate activities and potent stimulating diet is meant for the phlegm humor types.

Diet management for TYPE – K

As stated earlier, the three *rasas* (tastes) that are pungent, bitter and astringent are recommended to alleviate phlegm. Moreover, as against the basic properties of the phlegm humor, a *kapha* person's food should be somewhat rough, light, potent and hot. Most of the stimulating spices and condiments are favorable. *Kapha* is generally slow and steady, so is the digestion of this type of individual. Although *kapha* digestion is considered fairly sound, it takes more time. For this reason, this type of person needs to religiously avoid snacks. Likewise, overeating, even though infrequently might cause misery. Empty stomach is needed to move the products of digestion. It is therefore suggested that a TYPE – K maintain steady intervals between two meal types. Fasting is always beneficial.

Lifestyle management for TYPE – K

Long walks, running and exercise routines, participation in strenuous games like aerobics and swimming, avoiding sleeping during daytime and keeping awake till late hours, taking up wrestling and bodily fights are recommended. All sorts of physical work where the stored energy is used up are favourable for the TYPE - K personality.

Dry massaging the body with rough and coarse powder, gargles with pungent substances, use of rough bedclothes and overall living in dry environment would do well.

Keeping both physically as well as mentally occupied and strained is desired.

On the contrary, to remain at rest or in a state of inertia, both physically and mentally, would easily imbalance the humor. A TYPE - K person needs therefore to be on the go at all times. Ayurveda advocates that *kapha* people need to undertake optimal exercise and yoga, long brisk walks, pranayaam, strenuous sports like swimming, jogging, cycling, climbing, etc., that would help to use up needlessly conserved energy. Also so as to keep the mind alert, more often taking up mental tasks that would be challenging like puzzles, *sudoku*, or conditional mental stress and strain would do good (in contrast to TYPE - P who need to avoid the same). Lethargy in case of TYPE - K would generally not be due to being overworked as in case of the fire person, but quite the opposite due to little usage of the same. Using the stored energy in any and every form, even becoming more talkative is needed (although by nature the phlegm person dislikes being conversational and aggressive).

Sleep for a *kapha* person also has a lot of restrictions. Sleeping during daytime is completely forbidden (although the same is allowed to TYPE - V). This is simply because daytime naps are certain to cause *kapha* aggravation. Also early rising from the bed would be supportive. Especially as at the morning time (6 to 10 a.m.) *kapha* is naturally on the rise, so going against it is actually needed. It is fine if bedtime is somehow delayed.

Massage for the phlegm dominants is deep tissue and stimulating kind, mainly *kapha*, combating herb powder massage or simply dry massage.

As from the five senses, the sense of smell is *kapha*-defined, so intense and stimulating aroma oils may be used.

Meditation is also a necessity for *kapha* person, as it is for the *vatta* and *pitta* individuals. But it has to be consciously made sure that the posture remains erect and the *kapha* person does not go into a nap. Using some sort of fragrant and stimulating aromas as from *aggarbattis* (incense sticks) will do the job. Stimulation and warmth are the two indispensable credentials for balancing the *kapha* humor. This may be derived by taking warm, potent food, vigorous exercise routine and living in warm environment; other forms could be sun bathing, hot tub-bath, steam inhalation (*kapha* resides more in and above the chest), hot fomentation and poultice made from potent herbs like *ajwain, saunth,* etc., over the forehead. Ayurveda also recommends hot steam bath, using of intense nasal errhines (*nasya*) and gargles. Even the water used for drinking should be preferably warm with potent herbs and condiments boiled in it.

As for panchkarma therapy, *vamana* or inducing forceful vomiting is the best possible way to extract and aid to subside the phlegm stuck in the stomach, chest and throat region.

So as to balance *kapha,* the ancient text has approved following the regimen and daily routine as need to be done during the spring season.

IV. SELF-HELP GUIDE FOR TYPE – K

Diet

Diet that is heavy and unctuous, cold in action and more of sweet, salty and sour in taste would create imbalance in TYPE – K personality. One also needs to feast on less of milk and milk products. Similarly, fruit juices, cold drinks, ice creams and desserts and most sweeteners need to be restricted considerably. Although honey when taken in moderation or in small amounts would be beneficial. Occasionally, fasting on simple water or vegetable soup is needed. It has also to be kept in mind that owing to your slow digestion, you need to maintain a gap of approximately three hours between two meals. Night meals need to be taken early and *kapha* person would feel good if he avoids snacking in between the meals.

Tastes

Of the six tastes known to human tongue, TYPE - K person needs to feast more on pungent, bitter and astringent tastes and on purpose exclude more of sweet, salty and sour tastes in diet.

Herbs

All those herbs and kitchen ingredients that go against the basic traits of *kapha* would be definitely suitable for TYPE - K. This includes the herbs being light, rough, robust and hot in action. Also, the herbs that are bitter, pungent or astringent in taste or after-taste would be of help.

Four herbs, namely, holy basil, pepper, mint and asafoetida are particularly beneficial owing to the properties they possess. A number of more useful herbs have been detailed in the chart.

Condiments

Most of the condiments and spices used in our kitchens are beneficial for the TYPE - K people. Black pepper, ginger, garlic, turmeric, cumin, coriander, cinnamom, chillies, nutmeg, asafoetida, *ajwain*, fenugreek, mustard, etc. You may include roasted spicy *papad* in your daily diet as most of the *dals* and spices suit you as well as aid in keeping the gastric fire invigorated.

Vegetables

As a *kapha* person, you need to include more of bitter and pungent vegetables in your daily food. You may choice from ginger, garlic, turnip, peas, cabbage, carrots, beans, spinach, *methi*, bitter gourd, white gourd, etc. Only take less of watery vegetables like tomatoes, lemon and cucumber and also less of sour and salty pickles.

Fruits

Make your choice for less watery, less sweet or sour fruits. You may take more of dried fruits and slightly unripe fruits that have more astringent taste. Also you need to take fruit only in moderation and better still during the day hours.

Restricted diet

As a TYPE – K person, you need to be very limiting for the sweet, excessively salty and sour foods, oily, slimy, cold and heavy diets. More of desserts like ice-creams, *halwa*, Indian sweets, butter, fried snacks, cold drinks and stale foods may cause an unwanted aggravation of your inbuilt dosha.

Fasting for TYPE – K

As a *kapha* person, you tend to store energy in one form or the other; fasting for you should be no big deal and highly beneficial. You tend to be gifted with non-replenishing energy levels (owing to your favourite diet and lifestyle reserve), and for this reason you need to go on fasts more often. Once-a-week fasting is suggested when all you need to be taking is plain warm water. So as to settle your *kapha*, a little honey may be occasionally added to the same. If need be, you may take plain vegetable soup with *kapha*-suppressing spices like black pepper added to it. TYPE – K can surely gain from longer fasts especially during seasonal transition.

Essential oils

Basil oil is recommended. Inhalation of the same or gently rubbing a few drops onto the forehead helps to mitigate *kapha*.

Sleep pattern

Sleeping during daytime is a strict no-no for the *kapha* types. In case you fit straight into TYPE – K personality, then sleeping which is no doubt your favourite sport, needs to be trimmed down substantially. Morning 6 to 10 is the *kapha* activity time and has to be firmly followed so. Otherwise sleeping definitely is no problem with your type; it is the rising that needs to be prompted. There is something more that needs to be taken into consideration. As you are naturally gifted with coolness, it is more heat or warmth that is required by you. So while lying down for sleep, it would be suitable if you lie down on your left side. This promotes breathing through the right nostril and the warm *swara* or breath.

Exercise and Yoga for TYPE – K

All exercise routines may be more rightfully taken up during *kapha* activity time, between 6 and 10 a.m. or p.m. Most of the rigorous exercise is meant for TYPE – K. Some of the suggested yoga asanas are:

1. *Gomukh Asana*
2. *Bhujang Asana*
3. *Tada Asana*
4. *Katichakra Asana*
5. *Dhanur Asana*
6. *Nauka Asana*
7. *Shalabh Asana*

Some *pranayaam* or breathing techniques for TYPE – K

1. *Surya-bhedi Pranayaam*
2. *Bhastrika*
3. *Kapalbhati*

Mudra or hand alignment for TYPE - K

1. *Surya Mudra*
2. *Anjali Mudra*
3. *Linga Mudra*

Other highly beneficial yoga *kriyas* or methods for TYPE - K

1. *Kunjal Kriya*
2. *Jala Neti*
3. *Sutra Neti*
4. *Shankh Prakshalan*

Massage therapy

Strong and vigorous massage is your need with the use of massage techniques like friction, wringing, kneading and pressure-pressing movements. It would be better if the oil to be used is hot in potency like the mustard oil and better still if the oil is previously warmed. Although as TYPE - K is naturally supple with oiliness, using oil during massage should be restricted. Any form of deep tissue dry massage like the Ayurveda Udavartan is what you need.

Colour therapy

Imbibing bright and bold colours of yellow, orange and red is recommended. These may be used as clothes, room accessories like dim lights, curtain material, etc., reminisced during meditation or even on the walls of your room. Another way of absorbing the hot colours is to occasionally take in the charged water with the suggested colours. Although it has to be remembered that the red colour, being strongly searing, may sometimes cause considerable rise in your body temperature. It is therefore used externally as massage oil.

Gem therapy

External use of gem stones that are analogous to the suitable colours of red, orange and yellow would categorically suit the *kapha* person. TYPE – K personalities may go in for gems like the ruby, red coral and topaz. Also you need to limit using cooling gems like the moonstone, pearls and the diamond.

Meditation

Meditation helps in healing the soul, hence it is a must for your lifestyle. TYPE – K people tend to hold on to emotions, and meditation surely proves to be a virtue in the form of an outlet for you. You need not prolong the timings as you may lose interest and at the same time derive affluent outcome. You should take up the meditation schedule for as long as you can comfortably sit erect with eyes closed. Another suggestion is to concurrently use aromatic *aggarbattis* because it is the sense of smell that keeps you stimulated. Meditation is not really difficult for you owing to the stability trait of the *kapha* dosha which helps to keep the mind stable as well as focussed. The only commitment that you need here is to stay upright in the laze of the night. (Remember the mystic *vatta* time for meditation is between 2 and 6 a.m.).

Chakra balance

As in meditation, the TYPE – K individual who is a combination of the earth and water elements, needs to focus on and balance the same. The two chakras – Mooladhar and Swadhishthan – relate to earth and water respectively.

Mooladhar or the root chakra supports the earth element. This is red in colour and is located at the base of the spine. This chakra is said to be related to energy levels and physical stability.

Swadhishthan Chakra relates to the water element and is associated with the adrenals. This chakra is centred below the umbilicus and represents orange colour. It is believed to signify self-respect and bodily activity.

Seasonal support

During spring, there is natural aggravation of *kapha* dosha. Therefore the TYPE – K individual should take proper care during this season. You need to be more particular with your diet and lifestyle so as to stay clear of the twenty types of *kapha* maladies. Phlegm is believed to get accumulated in the early winters, as this is the time when water becomes cold, clear and heavy by nature. (This is in harmony with the properties of the phlegm humor.) Moreover, in summers, *kapha* is going to be naturally alleviated.

Suggested hobbies and career

All vigorous and energy-consuming hobbies are meant for the TYPE – K. This may include sports like swimming, cycling, tennis, mountaineering, etc., although you might feel more at home with gardening and rafting which makes you one with either the earth or water.

As far as livelihood is concerned, your caring and compassionate nature would be at ease in case you could take up some job in management, counselling, tourism, doctoring and nursing or even teaching, or all that seems to work-up your latent mind and body energy reservoir would do you good.

Important Norms

The best suggested norm for a *kapha* person or the TYPE – K individual would be to use your energy, mainly because you have plenty.

V. HERBS AS HEALERS

Kapha-subsiding herbs

Holy Basil

The herb of holy basil or *tulsi* as it is commonly known in India, is rough and light by nature, bitter and pungent in taste, and leaves a bitter after-taste. Being hot in potency, basil helps to decrease the aggravated *kapha* (phlegm). It is likewise beneficial for *vatta* individuals.

Basil has anti-toxic as well as antibacterial properties. Juice of the leaves is useful for bronchitis, respiratory allergies, coryza and other *kapha*-related maladies. It mainly works as an expectorant assisting in the removal of excess phlegm.

TYPE – K individuals may benefit immensely using this herb. Fresh leaves of tulsi may be masticated alone and the juice taken in slowly. These when consumed along with some black pepper works better. Honey can also be added to it in moderate quantity.

Tulsi leaves may be taken daily boiled in tea or as decoction prepared along with a pinch of ground cloves, pepper and cinnamon. This helps keep the *kapha* cold away.

Pepper *(Kali Mirch)*

This is another herb which is a natural boon for the *kapha* imbalance. Colds and cough may be easily kept at bay by regular intake of two or three black peppers everyday.

Many respiratory afflictions relating to increased phlegm benefit by frequent use of this herb. Approximately half a teaspoon of kali mirch powder can be boiled in a glass full of milk or added to the decoction of daily tea. This provides great relief in case of running nose and recurrent sneezing, bouts of cough, allergic rhinitis. Freshly ground kali mirch can be added to mishri and ghee in equal quantities and sucked slowly for extraction of the dried phlegm.

Also slowly chewing and sucking on the juice of pepper along with some mishri is beneficial for sore throat and hoarseness of voice.

Merely daily intake of ground pepper powder mixed with honey is a sure support for the *kapha* individuals.

Mint

Mint is bitter in taste as well as after-taste. It is hot in potency and light, rough and robust in nature. Thus being bitter, rough, hot in potency and also robust by nature, Ayurveda advocates the herb to be a destroyer of aggravated *kapha* or the phlegm body humor.

The leaves of mint either in raw form or prepared into a chutney is extremely beneficial for those suffering from *kapha*-related stomach disorders like loss of hunger, indigestion, occasional nausea and even worm infestation.

Kapha imbalance triggers off respiratory distress easily. Here again the herb comes as aid. Mint contains a unique property of extracting and decreasing phlegm. Some juice may be extracted by crushing fresh mint leaves. This may be added to equal quantity of ginger juice. Five to ten ml of the mixture is to be taken twice a day along with honey. The use of mint is also advisable for asthmatic patients.

In the cases of non-specific diarrhoea and vomiting which could have been a result of food poisoning, mint again comes to the rescue. This owes to the fact that mint contains anti-toxic properties. A paste can be prepared by pounding together mint leaves and onions. One to two teaspoons of the same can be taken three to four times in a day.

As earlier stated, the *kapha* humor is naturally on the rise in early childhood. For babies and small children showing digestion problems like flatulence, diminished hunger, recurrent colds, relapsing fevers and occasional nausea, the herb of mint may be used. A decoction may be prepared by boiling mint leaves, basil leaves, ginger, large cardamom, a pinch of asafoetida and some crushed black pepper. One or two teaspoons can be given two to three times with some mishri or honey added to it.

Being hot and robust, mint is also a supportive herb for *vatta* imbalance.

Asafoetida (*Hing*)

Hing is believed to be light, slimy and robust in nature. Asafoetida is bitter in taste and also leaves a bitter after-taste. Its potency is hot, thus it is generally used in treating the disorders in which there is aggravation of *kapha* body humor or when the fire inside the body systems remains dwindled. Being hot and slimy it also suits *vatta* imbalance. Stimulant, expectorant, carminative and antispasmodic are some of the qualities of this herb. The dosage is approximately 125 to 500 mg. Other than this, according to Ayurvedic texts, the specific actions of asafoetida are summarised by the following terms:

1. *Ruchya* – that which causes longing for food
2. *Deepana* – that which invigorates the gastric fire for digestion of food
3. *Pachhana* – that which is digestive
4. *Anulomana* – as it subsides the excessive wind
5. *Shoolprashmana* – that which combats pain
6. *Krimighana* – acts as a wormicide and
7. *Hridya* – it is beneficial for the heart.

External application of asafoetida on the umbilicus in case of abdominal discomfort caused by flatulence is of great help in infants and small children. Similarly in respiratory disorders like bronchitis, cough and cold, the local massaging of the chest helps. The smoke that results from burning hing can be inhaled so as to get relief from spasms of bronchial asthma.

The benefits of asafoetida have been also emphasised in the metabolic as well as nervous disorders like paralysis, sciatica, lockjaw or insomnia relating to *vatta* imbalance. Yet, it is required to be used with caution in case you are a possessor of hot temperament or even in hot climate conditions. So, *pitta* individuals need to minimise its intake.

Part Two

PHYSIQUE AND TEMPERAMENT OF HUMOR TYPES

S. No.	Physical Features & Mental Temperament	TYPE – V	TYPE – P	TYPE – K
1	**Body appearance**	Thin, lean body	Sensitive and proportionate body	Full and symmetrical body, tendency of obesity
2	**Skin colour**	Blackish	Yellowish or reddish	Fair complexion
3	**Skin appearance**	Dry, rough and cracked skin with swollen and visible veins	Pimples, moles, freckles etc. and reddish lips, ears, hands, etc.	Slimy, smooth, soft and oily skin
4	**Hair texture**	Rough, hard and brittle hair	Sparse hair growth and premature greying and hair falling	Thick, black and greasy hair, maybe curly
5	**Eyes**	Dusky and sunken eyes with blackish tinge	Yellow or red coloured	White and lubricous
6	**Mouth**	Dry	Dry and burning sensation	Excess production and secretion of phlegm
7	**Tongue**	Dry, fissured, blackish and stained	Reddish colour with black tinge and ulcerated	White, moist and coated
8	**Taste**	Astringent and distorted	Bitter and sour	Sweet taste in mouth

S. No.	Physical Features & Mental Temperament	TYPE – V	TYPE – P	TYPE – K
9	**Voice**	Cracked and heavy pitch	Clear speech	Sweet and impressive
10	**Thirst**	Misleading and unclear	More or excessive	Less
11	**Hunger**	Hunger pattern and digestion keeps varying	Good digestive power and more hunger	Less hunger, feeling of fullness after food
12	**Sweat**	Less and without smell	More, hot and smelly	Normal and cold
13	**Urine**	Slightly yellowish with blue tinge	Yellowish and hot, perhaps with red tinge	Whitish, thick and frothy, somewhat slimy
14	**Faeces**	Less frequent, constipated, hard, dark and fragile	Loose, hot, smelly and with burning sensation	Solid and slimy, perhaps with mucous
15	**Nails**	Rough, blackish and dry	Reddish or yellowish	White and unctuous
16	**Gait**	Fast	Normal	Slow
17	**Dreams**	Flying in the skies	Fire, flame, candles, sun, lightning, stars	Sea, rivers, waterfall, lotus, etc.
18	**Sleep pattern**	Less sleep	Less or normal sleep	More sleep, lethargy

S. No.	Physical Features & Mental Temperament	TYPE – V	TYPE – P	TYPE – K
19	**Natural manifestation**	There is intolerance for cold foods and cold temperature. Anything warm to hot comforts	Colder climate, cold and sweetened foods are amiable	Aversion for cold which is uncomfortable. Liking for hot foods and environment
20	**Nature**	Impulsive, impatient, hasty, hyper, fast, short tempered, indecisive, cowardly, creative, manipulative	Hot-tempered, irritating, logical, intelligent, witty, brave, clever, ascetic, obsessive	Sober, patient, humble, stable, tolerant, unexcited, calm and composed, disciplined, lazy and slow
21	**Pulse**	Zigzag, fast and irregular	Impulsive, heavy and jumping	Smooth, weak and slow
22	**Diseases**	80 types	40 types	20 types
24	**Intolerance for**	Cold	Heat	Cold

RECREATING THE BALANCE

Diet	TYPE - V	TYPE - P	TYPE - K
Favourable Tastes	Sweet, salty and sour	Sweet, bitter and astringent	Pungent, bitter and astringent
Properties	Warm, nourishing, unctuous	Cold, bland, mild and heavy	Hot, potent and light
Action	Hot	Cold	Hot
Fruits	Apples, bananas, papayas, grapes	Less of citrus fruits like lemon, orange, etc.	Less to moderate, only in daytime
Vegetables	Less of ground tubers, take less raw vegetables	Mostly gourds, cucumber, spinach, green leafy vegetables	Mostly gourds, onion, ginger, garlic, radish. Less potatoes
Cereals	Red rice, wheat, black gram, ragi	Red rice, wheat, barley, *sooji*, oats	Wheat, oats, less of rice, black gram
Drinks	Buttermilk, warm soup	Fruit juices, cold drinks, coconut water	Hot and spiced soup, water boiled with ginger, pepper, lemon. Add honey
Milk products	Curd, *paneer*, butter, buttermilk, ghee	Ghee is good	Only in moderation
Spices and condiments	Moderate intake	Less	More is needed
Kitchen herbs	Asafoetida, large cardamom, fennel	Less of garlic, asafoetida	Holy basil, curry leaves, mint
Pulses	In moderation, avoid Bengal gram	Avoid horse-gram and flat beans	Mostly good
Dry fruits and nuts	Very little	In moderation	Less

Diet	TYPE - V	TYPE - P	TYPE - K
Sweets	Fine	Desserts from sugarcane juice, powdered jaggery (*shakkar*)	Honey is advised
Fats	Oil, ghee, butter	Ghee in moderation. Less of mustard, gingerly oils	Less
Diet to avoid	Dry and cold foods, carbonated drinks, unripe fruit	Hot, spicy foods and wines	Cold, creamy foods, desserts, carbonated and frozen foods
Diet intake pattern	Eat small meals but frequently	Sustain normal blood sugar, eat regularly	Maintain proper gaps for slow digestion

FAVOURABLE LIFESTYLE

Sleep pattern	Sleep pattern needs to be organised and strictly followed.	Avoid lights at bedtime, sleep more relaxed. Sleep on right side.	Day sleep is strictly forbidden. Sleep on left side.
Exercise and Yoga	Follow routine. *Bhastrika, kapalbhati* and alternate deep breathing helps.	*Sheetali* and *sheetkari pranayaams* are cooling. Deep breathing through left nostril.	All *pranayaams* vigorously. Deep breathing through right nostril.
Sex life	Desire and energy needs to be saved.	Not too vigorous.	Moderate to good.
Emotional support	Take up a gentle hobby to remain distracted from unnecessary apprehensions.	Spend time with friends who are not competition to you.	Be more talkative with friends where you can relieve and give vent to emotions.
Massage therapy	Needs to be followed religiously, warming oils are suitable.	Compassionate massage with soothing and cooling oil, crème.	Stimulating, deep tissue or dry massage.
Aroma therapy	Lavender, saffron, cinnamon.	Sandalwood, rose, jasmine	Basil, eucalyptus oils
Color therapy	Green color	Blue, violet, indigo.	Yellow, red, orange.
Panchkarma techniques	*Vasti* (Enemas)	*Virechana* (Purgation)	*Vamana* (Vomiting)
Remedial diet	Oil	Ghee	Honey
Seasonal intervention	More care during Rainy season which vitiates *vatta*	Autumn vitiates *pitta* so needs more concern.	Spring vitiates *kapha* and needs more care.
Important message	Follow routine	De-stress occasionally	Utilise the stored energy

HERBS AS HEALERS

Herb	*Vatta*	*Pitta*	*Kapha*
Aamla	Decrease	Decrease	Decrease
Ajwain	Decrease	Increase	Decrease
Aloe vera	–	Decrease	Decrease
Asafoetida	Decrease	Increase	Decrease
Asparagus	Decrease	Decrease	–
Betel	Decrease	Increase	Decrease
Bilva	Decrease	–	Decrease
Black pepper	Decrease	–	Decrease
Bramhi	–	Decrease	Decrease
Camphor	Decrease	Decrease	Decrease
Cardamom	Decrease	Decrease	Decrease
Catechu	–	Decrease	Decrease
Cinnamom	Decrease	–	Decrease
Clove	–	Decrease	Decrease
Coconut	Decrease	Decrease	–
Coriander	Decrease	Decrease	Decrease
Fennel	Decrease	Decrease	–
Garlic	Decrease	–	Decrease
Ginger	Decrease	–	Decrease
Grapes	Decrease	Decrease	–
Greater Cardamom	Decrease	Increase	Decrease
Groundnut	Decrease	–	–
Harad	Decrease	Decrease	Decrease
Henna	–	Decrease	Decrease
Isabgol	Decrease	Decrease	–
Jamun	Increase	Decrease	Decrease
Karela	–	Decrease	Decrease
Lemon	Decrease	Increase	Decrease
Liquorice	Decrease	Decrease	

Herb	*Vatta*	*Pitta*	*Kapha*
Lotus	–	Decrease	Decrease
Mango	Decrease	Decrease	–
Methi	Decrease	–	–
Mint	Decrease	–	Decrease
Mustard	Decrease	–	Decrease
Neem	–	Decrease	Decrease
Nutmeg	Decrease	–	Decrease
Onion	Decrease	Increase	–
Papaya	Decrease	–	Decrease
Pomegranate	Decrease	Decrease	Decrease
Rose	Decrease	Decrease	
Saffron	Decrease	Decrease	Decrease
Sandalwood	–	Decrease	Decrease
Sugarcane	Decrease	Decrease	Decrease
Tulsi	Decrease	Decrease	–
Turmeric	Decrease	Decrease	Decrease
White gourd (Ripe)	Decrease	Decrease	Decrease

SELF-IDENTIFICATION QUESTIONNAIRE

Your Physical Characteristics

1. Your Body Structure
   a. lean with light bones
   b. medium weight with stout bony frame
   c. large frame and heavy bones

2. Weight
   a. normally less or underweight
   b. medium-sized or slightly hefty
   c. heavy or tendency to gain weight

3. Height
   a. either very tall or very short
   b. average height
   c. proportionally well-built in height-weight ratio

4. Your Skin Type
   a. rough skin devoid of much fat, prominent veins
   b. soft, warm, oily skin tends to glow
   c. smooth, thick, cool, moist or oily

5. Muscles
   a. underdeveloped muscles
   b. well developed
   c. plump and fleshy kind

6. Teeth and Nails
   a. uneven teeth with gaps, fragile nails
   b. tooth decay and bleeding gums, smooth nails
   c. large, strong teeth, gums and nails

7. Skin Complexion
   a. darkish and easy tanning
   b. fair with reddish radiance, more freckles
   c. pale, tans slowly

8. Your Hair
   a. dry, curly or wavy hair, early baldness
   b. thin hair, early greying
   c. thick, black and normally heavy and oily

9. Your Eyes
   a. small-sized, somewhat dull
   b. medium size, copper tinge, prone to redness
   c. big, white and shiny eyes

10. Your Voice
    a. hoarse, low-pitched
    b. deep, penetrating voice
    c. low-pitched and pleasant

11. Your Movement (Pace)
    a. fast, jump to conclusions
    b. steady, sturdy and controlled
    c. slow and intentional

12. Your Appetite
    a. variable, sometimes good, sometimes too bad
    b. aggressive, have to be fed on time
    c. mostly good, but can be controlled

13. Your Digestion
    a. often erratic
    b. good and easy
    c. slow, takes time

14. Defecation
    a. gassy, hard and towards constipation
    b. regular, somewhat loose, sometimes with burning sensation
    c. bulky, slow and sometimes with mucous

15. Your Stamina
    a. usually poor, wastes energy
    b. good, but tends to over-exert
    c. good, conserves energy

16. Your Sex Drive
    a. desire is more, less energy
    b. strong desire, adequate energy
    c. less to reasonable desire, steady energy

17. Your Reaction
    a. drastic and impulsive
    b. planned but firm, abrupt
    c. slow and passive

18. Your Lifestyle
    a. irregular, impulsive
    b. balanced, organised and busy
    c. static and rigid, sedentary

19. Ailments You Generally Experience
    a. body aches, joint pains, debility
    b. skin afflictions, burning sensation
    c. phlegm is more, ENT problems

20. Your Habits and Comforts
    a. incessant planning, full of ideas, comfortable with like-minded, and music
    b. putting plans into action, monopolising conversation, approval is comforting
    c. keeps work going well, peaceful attitude

Your Mental Characteristics

1. Your Memory Power
    a. forgets soon, long-term memory is less

   b. sharp recall
   c. holds on to long-term memories

2. Your Mental Ability
   a. Lots of ideas and keep changing mind
   b. Gather a lot of facts before forming opinion
   c. Mind made up quickly, does not change often

3. Your Dominant Emotion
   a. anxiety and fear
   b. challenging, judgmental, easily angered
   c. materialistic, sometimes greedy and possessive

4. Your Grasping Power
   a. fast to grasp, but cannot hold on
   b. good at grasping, only when interested
   c. slow learner but steady understanding

5. Your Socialising
   a. overall trust is less
   b. makes easy friends, sometimes challenging
   c. stable relationships

6. Climate That Comforts You
   a. warm, towards humid
   b. colder climate
   c. hot weather

7. Ability of Forbearance
   a. incoherent and tends to grieve
   b. immediately frenzied, but cools down soon
   c. capable of sustaining painful conditions with calm

8. Ability to Manage Jobs
   a. Good at getting things started, but not finishing them
   b. Organised, manages a task from start to end
   c. Start takes time and motivation, accomplishing is easy

9. Animal to Whom You Bear Resemblance
   a. a crow
   b. a cat
   c. a cow

10. Prominent Dreams
   a. nightmares, grieving or flying in skies
   b. violence, transforming from one state to another, fire
   c. water, everyday events, mountains

11. Sleeping Pattern
   a. getting to sleep not easy, random
   b. sleeps quick, but light
   c. normal pattern

12. Waking Up
   a. wake up tired
   b. wake up alert, spontaneous
   c. heavy, difficult to wake up

13. Your Beliefs and Preferances
   a. constant planner, but unpredictable
   b. executes ideas with firmness and stability
   c. peacemaker, invariable beliefs

14. What Calms Your Nerves
   a. sense of security
   b. affection and judgmental balance
   c. understanding and stability

15. Your Worst Temperament
   a. impulsive, ungrateful and easily jealous
   b. hot-tempered, criticising and challenging
   c. hard to change beliefs, stubborn, egoistic, unwavering hostility

16. Performance Under Stress
    a. easily excited when under stress
    b. angry or critical under stress
    c. easy going, not easily stressed.

17. Your Basic Personality Trait
    a. creative and imaginative
    b. smart, efficient and perfectionist
    c. caring, calm and tolerant

18. Tastes You Like More
    a. pungent and salty
    b. salty and sour
    c. sweet and sour

Now after you have marked it for yourself, you need to sum up. It is suggested that you take into consideration in totality both bodily as well as mental attributes. In case there are more of **a.**s you have dominance of *vatta* in your system, and this makes you TYPE - V personality. Similarly more of **b.**s or **c.**s would define your persona as TYPE - P and TYPE - K respectively. Many a times there may be presence of two or even all the three doshas within you; in that case, you need to concentrate more on what is evidently dominant in your basic physical constitution.

YOGA AND BREATHING TECHNIQUES

Yoga Kriyas

Kunjal

Fill the belly with warm water. Then stand, keep left hand on the belly and gently rub the first three fingers of the right hand at the back of the tongue. This would cause the water to gush out just as vomitus.

Jala Neti

Previously warmed salty water is made to enter that nostril through which the breath is being inhaled. For this purpose a small kettle like vessel is generally used. The water is made to enter from one nostril and the head is made to tilt onto the other side so as to make easy escape of the water from the other nostril.

Sutra Neti

A *sutra* or fine-thread string is dipped into hot water or milk (for TYPE – P) and is made to enter that very nostril through which the breath is being inhaled. As it enters the throat, the sutra is slowly pulled out through the mouth with the help of middle and index fingers.

Shankh Prakshalana

This yoga technique supports cleansing of the entire digestive system. Herein at first 2 to 3 glassful of warmed and salted water is to be taken. Subsequently, some important asanas, viz., *Bhujangasana*, *Urdhva hastottanasana*, *Katichakra Asana* and *Udarakarsha Asana* are performed. The whole process is repeated to the time there is proper faecal evacuation.

Trataka

This is mind-concentration yoga technique where the eye vision is made to be focussed on some article like a candle flame. The process of staring at the object without blinking the eyes is to be maintained till the time eyes begin to water.

Yoga Asanas

Padma Asana

This is the lotus pose wherein at first you sit cross-legged and then place both feet on the opposite thigh. The neck and spine must be upright.

Siddha Asana

This is a sitting asana that teaches a person to comfortably sit at one place for long. Sitting down with back straight, first the left leg is bent at the knee and folded with pressing it against the left thigh. Repeat the same with the right leg. In the process, both the heels are set tightly against the seam of the perineum.

Bhujanga Asana

Lie on your stomach keeping both the hands below the shoulders and the feet are joined at the back. Then slowly breathe in and lift your waist upwards and backwards as much as possible. This asana gives the shape of a snake to the body.

Trikon Asana

First stand straight and keep a distance of approximately two feet between the legs. Then turn left stretching the right arm over the head to touch the right ear. Try touching your left foot with the left hand. Then repeat the same process in the right direction.

Kati-chakra Asana

Stand erect with both feet apart by approximately one feet distance. Extend both arms forward at shoulder length. Now breathe in and turn sideways as much as possible, with the legs kept straight. Then come back to the original position and exhale. Repeat the same in the other direction.

Pavanmukta Asana

Lie straight on the back with both feet joined. Then slowly raise the left leg, folding it at the knee and bring it to the chest. Now try and touch the knee of the folded leg to the nose lifting your head forwards. In the process the right leg remains straight. Then repeat the complete process with the right leg.

Dhanur Asana

Lying on the stomach, try holding the ankles of your feet folded at the knees, with the stretched arms at the back. This asana is rightly acclaimed as the bow posture.

Gomukh Asana

Sit straight on the left leg folded at the knee. Fold the right leg over the left leg. Thereafter, the right arm should be taken up and turned at the back with the elbow joint touching the back of the head. Try to hold the fingers of right hand with that of the left on the back.

Nauka Asana

Lie flat on your stomach with arms stretched forwards and both feet joined. Then slowly breathe in and lift the hands and feet upwards simultaneously making the body look like a boat. Thus this is referred to as the boat pose.

Shalabh Asana

Lie down on the stomach and join the feet together and both hands on the ground. Subsequently lift your body upwards from the feet to the waist till the body weight comes on the stomach. This gives the shape of a locust to the body.

Tada Asana

Stand erect with both feet joined. Breathe in and extend both arms upwards with hands clasped and facing the sky. Stretch upwards as much as possible. Now release the breath and come back to original position.

Pranayaam Techniques

Bhastrika

You need at first to sit comfortably in easy asana position like Sukhasana or the Padamasana and then the breathing technique is performed. The breath is inhaled deeply into the lungs and then exhaled through both nostrils. It may be repeated a number of times.

Kapalbhati

This technique is believed to create glow on the forehead. While sitting in asana position, the breath that is being exhaled is made to puff out with force. Also the stomach moves in automatically as the breath is being released.

Anulom Vilom

This is a type of alternate deep breathing. Both the nostrils are made to be closed one after the other. You may start with first pressing your right nostril with your right thumb and inhaling through the left nostril. Subsequently, the left nostril is pressed by the ring finger and middle finger of the right hand while the breath is exhaled via the right nostril. The same process is then repeated with the left nostril.

Suryabhedi Pranayaam

This is a warming pranayaam technique in which deep breath is inhaled through the right nostril and released via the left nostril.

Chanderbhedi Pranayaam

This is a cooling breathing technique while is quite favourable for the *pitta* types. In this exercise the breath is mainly drawn in through the left nostril and exhaled through the right nostril.

Bhramari Pranayaam

The eyes are closed and breath is taken in. The hands are brought near the ears and the fingers are positioned in such a way that the thumb closes both ear cavities, index finger rests on the forehead and the rest three fingers are made to cover the eyelids. Then, while exhaling through the nostrils try producing the sound like a bee and keep your inner focus on the crown chakra.

Sheetali Pranayaam

This is another body cooling breathing exercise wherein sitting in asana position, the tongue is first made to be folded like a tube and air is gulped in through the mouth and the tongue. Then the mouth is closed and the breath is released through the two nostrils.

Shitkari Pranayaam

The tongue is at first made to touch the upper inner side of the mouth cavity and the teeth are joined together. With the lips kept open, air is to be drawn in through the lips producing a peculiar hissing sound. Then the mouth is to be closed and the breath is made to exhale via the two nostrils.

Mudras or the Hand-Alignment Techniques

Gyana Mudra

This alignment is formed by touching the tip of the thumb with that of the index finger. There is no particular time limit constraint for this mudra.

Prana Mudra

This mudra is formed when the tips of ring finger and the small finger together come in proximity and touch the tip of the thumb. This mudra also has no time restrictions.

Surya Mudra

Here, the ring finger is made to settle down at the root of the thumb, with the thumb exerting a little pressure on the same. As this alignment tends to increase warmth in the body systems, it is generally recommended to be practised for fifteen to twenty minutes daily.

Vayu Mudra

This particular mudra is also called a pain-killer. For this alignment, you need to place the tip of your index finger in the root of the thumb and allow the thumb to press it mildly. This may be practised as long as there seems to be *vatta* imbalance.

Apan Vayu Mudra

This mudra results from first joining together of the middle and ring fingers and then the joined tips of both the fingers are made to touch the tip of the thumb. This must be practised frequently with no time bar.

Varuna Mudra

When the tip of the little finger is made to touch the tip of the thumb, Varuna Mudra is created. This is in general moisturising and soothing for the body. You may put it into practice as and when needed.

Anjali Mudra

When the right hand is made to rest on the palm of the left hand

and this alignment is kept on the lap, then this mudra comes into being. This is particularly de-stressing when practised just before sleep.

Linga Mudra

This is another warming hand arrangement which may be crafted by amalgamation of the fingers of both the hands; and the thumb of the left hand is kept straight up in the process.

Shoonya Mudra

This mudra is formed mainly by folding the middle finger and making it touch the root of thumb. The thumb should slightly press on the same.

Hridya Mudra

This hand alignment is highly beneficial for the heart and thus its name. The index finger is first folded and kept at the root of the thumb. Then the middle and ring finger are joined and their tips are together made to touch the tip of the thumb.

Glossary

Aahara	:	Diet
Aakasha	:	Denotes ether or the sky, which is one of the five basic natural elements that make up the entire natural existence.
Aggarbattis	:	Incense sticks
Ayurveda	:	The age old science of life and longevity.
Dhatus	:	Body tissues
Dosha	:	The three body humors or the bio-regulatory principles of the body.
Drava	:	Liquid
Guna	:	Basic trait or the natural attribute
Guru	:	Heavy
Humor	:	The three bio-regulatory principles, viz., air, fire and phlegm in the body as recognized by Ayurveda.
Jala	:	Denotes water and is one of the five basic natural elements that make up the entire natural existence.
Kapha	:	Phlegm body humor which is the bio-regulatory principle that sources formation, nutrition and sustenance of the physical body.

Khara	:	Rough
Laghu	:	Light
Mahabhootas	:	Basic elements
Nasya	:	Nasal errhines, use of medicine by nasal route.
Panchbhoota	:	The five natural basic elements or the fundamental building blocks, viz., ether, air, fire, water and earth.
Panchkarma	:	The prime five cleansing processes of the body, viz., inducing vomiting, purgation, enemas and nasal errhines.
Pichhila	:	Slimy or greasy
Pitta	:	Fire humor of the body which attributes to the process of physiological activities of metabolism, assimilation, digestion, etc., in the body.
Prakriti	:	The natural physical constitution and mental temperament of an individual.
Prithvi	:	Denotes the earth and is one of the five basic natural elements that make up the entire natural existence.
Rajas Guna	:	Variable and erratic mental attribute.
Ruksha	:	Dry
Sara	:	Fluid
Satvic	:	Relating to positive mental state.
Satwa	:	Natural essence
Satwa Guna	:	Positive and balanced mental state.
Saunth	:	Dry ginger powder
Shakha	:	Extremities
Shita	:	Cold or cool
Shloka	:	Ancient Sanskrit adage

Slakshma	:	Smooth
Snigdha	:	Oily, unctuous
Srotas	:	Channels.
Sthira	:	Static
Sthula	:	Heavy, gross
Sukshma	:	Minute
Tamas Guna	:	Negative and depressed state of the mind.
Tejas	:	Denotes the fire and is one of the five basic natural elements that make up the entire natural existence.
Tikshana	:	Sharp
Tridosha	:	The three body humors, viz., air, fire and phlegm.
Ushana	:	Hot
Vamana	:	Vomiting
Vasti	:	Enema
Vatta	:	Air body humor that is the product of ether and air and manifests as moving bio-regulatory principle in human body.
Vayu	:	Denotes the air which is one of the five basic natural elements that make up the entire natural existence.
Vihara	:	Everyday lifestyle
Virechana	:	Purgation
Vishada	:	Transparent or clear
Vishamagni	:	Disrupted gastric fire

Index